FRIEND OF ANIMALS

Illustrated by
PAUL BROWN

FRIEND OF ANIMALS
The Story of Henry Bergh

by

Mildred Mastin Pace

Edited and with an Introduction by
Danny L. Miller

The Jesse Stuart Foundation
Ashland, Kentucky
1995

FRIEND OF ANIMALS
The Story of Henry Bergh

Copyright © 1942 by Charles Scribner's Sons
Copyright © 1970 by Mildred Mastin Pace
Copyright © 1995 by the Jesse Stuart Foundation

Book Design by FLEXISOFT

Library of Congress Cataloging-in-Publication Data

Pace, Mildred Mastin.
  Friend of animals : the story of Henry Bergh / by Mildred Mastin Pace ; edited and with an introduction by Danny L. Miller ; illustrated by Paul Brown.
      p.   cm.
  Originally published: New York : C. Scribner's Sons, 1942.
  Summary: A biography of a man instrumental in having laws passed in nineteenth-century United States to protect animals and chidren from cruelty.
  ISBN 0-945084-47-1
  1. Bergh, Henry, 1811-1888--juvenile literature. 2. Animals, Treatment of--Juvenile literature.   [1. Bergh, Henry, 1811-1888. 2. American Society for the Prevention of Cruelty to Animals--History. 3. Animals--Treatment. 4. Reformers.] I. Miller, Danny L. II. Brown, Paul, 1893-1958, ill. III. Title.
  HV4764.P3   1995
  179' .3'092--dc20
  [B]   94-47532
                                                                   CIP
                                                                    AC

The Jesse Stuart Foundation
P.O. Box 391 Ashland, KY 41114
1995

CONTENTS

Dedicated to

Kathleen Beyer Dorman
September 24, 1953
October 21, 1991

_____

Contributions to the
Kathy Beyer Dorman Fund, which provides
books for adult new readers can be made to:

Kathy Beyer Dorman Fund
C/o Jesse Stuart Foundation
P.O. Box 391
Ashland, KY 41114

INTRODUCTION

When I first started to edit <u>Henry Bergh: Friend of Animals</u>, the Jesse Stuart Foundation's third book in its series for junior and adult new readers, I had never heard the name Henry Bergh. Sure, I had heard of the ASPCA, the American Society for the Prevention of Cruelty to Animals. I would say that almost everyone in the United States has heard of this organization. But few of us have heard of the founder of this important and influential Society.

We might think that the founding of the ASPCA would have been an easy thing, that most people would be in favor of humane treatment of animals. But, as the reader of this book will learn, it was not easy. Like all great achievements, it took a dedicated and committed leader to accomplish the goal. Henry Bergh is an inspirational figure. He gave his life to a cause that he believed in: opposition to cruelty to animals. His life was one of sacrifice and focus. He was called names and made fun of. But he never gave up his beliefs.

It is quite fitting, I believe, for the Jesse Stuart Foundation to republish this work by Mildred Mastin Pace. Jesse Stuart loved nature and animals. All of his writings are filled with references to the beauty of nature, and many of his works have animals in them, such as the snakes in each story in the collection <u>Dawn of Remembered Spring</u>. In an unpublished essay entitled "Animal Personalities," he wrote, "Each horse and mule had a personality. He or she was a living animal."

I have learned a great deal about the animal (and child) welfare movements in the United States from reading this book. I have also learned about many other things, such as the transportation system in New York in the late 1800s and P. T. Barnum and the circus/museum industry during the same time period. This book is exciting to read, as well as informative. I was interested from the beginning to the end, and I believe every reader will feel the same.

Danny L. Miller
Northern Kentucky University

ONE

SHIP BUILDER'S SON

The crowds began to gather early in the day. By eleven in the morning, Henry found it increasingly difficult, with excitement boiling all around him, to wait quietly on the lawn.

The front lawn was a pleasant enough place on an ordinary day. From where he sat, Henry could see the square-rigged ships, and brigs and barques, that filled New York's lower East Side riverfront. He could look down across the slope of grass, past the poplars that lined the water's edge, and watch the boat traffic up and down the river. He could see, too, Baptizin' Beach, where he and his brother Christian swam, and the yellow curve of sandy shore where they played.

Best of all, he could see his father's shipyard. From it now came the shouts of men, the ringing of hammers, the noise of boards dropping, the whine of saws.

These sounds had awakened Henry at daybreak. On most days they would never have roused him, he was so used to them. But on this morning the most familiar things became strange and different, charged with excitement.

For this was the day of a launching. Today the Paris, a schooner built by his father, would slip down the ways into the water for the first time.

The Bergh yards had never built a bigger or a finer ship. She weighed three hundred and eighty-eight tons, and her launching was an event all New York anticipated.

"Give us a hand, Henry, lad," a workman called from the veranda, "We want to hustle these chairs out onto the lawn." Henry ran toward him, glad to be busy.

There had been nothing but hustle at the Bergh home for three days past. The heavy frame house had shaken with activity: the constant coming and going of tradesmen; servant girls cleaning and scrubbing and polishing till everything shone; extra help busy in the kitchen; and throughout the house the tantalizing aroma of hams and turkeys roasting, of cakes and pies cooling from the oven.

By the time the chairs were out, Henry saw that carriages already filled Scammell and Water Streets.

Launching time could not be far off. The crowd along the waterfront was growing by the minute.

The many voices merged into a steady roar, and above the roar Henry could hear guards shouting, "Stand back!. . . Can't ya see the ropes? . . . Get back, please. . . . We don't want nobody to get hurt."

Suddenly Henry realized that the building noises at the shipyard had stopped. The men had quit work! He stood tense, waiting until he heard the bell ring. That was the signal for all to gather.

At the sound, his mother, usually so calm and quiet, came hurrying out of the house. The servants, rushed and excited, followed her.

Henry wanted to run as fast as he could down the lawn, through Water Street to the dock. Christian was there already. As he was older than Henry, his father had let him spend the morning at the yards. Mrs. Bergh smiled down at the boy and said, "There's really no great hurry, you know. Father won't launch the <u>Paris</u> without me."

At the dock a band played and flags and streamers blazed in the sun. Orders were called from the ship to the toiling men below; answers were yelled back to the ship.

Henry glanced at his father's tense face, and wished the preliminaries would soon be over. Many dangers threatened a launching, and until it was safely accomplished, not only his father but the workmen too were tense and anxious.

A few months before, a ship launched at another yard had swung around when she hit the water and smashed into the dock. Two men were killed and a dozen injured. The memory of it made Henry a little sick. He tried not to think of it.

Then he saw the Paris quiver. The crowd silenced, as if every person in it held his breath. There was a screech as the ship pushed down the ways, and then a great splash. She stood straight and proud in the water, and the cheer that rose was heard for miles!

Men shouted hurrahs, and women waved their handkerchiefs. Carpenters, caulkers, joiners, even the apprentices joyfully slapped each other on the back. Henry's father, smiling now, shook hands with the shipowner for whom he had built the Paris, and people rushed up with congratulations.

The ship sailed gracefully down the river toward the sea. "No more work today," Mr. Bergh called to the yard boss. "This time is a time for celebrating." More cheers went up as this announcement was relayed. The men all knew, too, that Mr. Bergh would provide plenty of punch for them that afternoon, and lots of good food to go with it. So smooth and successful a launching demanded a celebration.

Back at the Bergh home, visitors streamed onto the lawns. Henry's mother smiled as she moved among the guests, pretty as a flower in her sprigged muslin dress. But it was his father who dominated the bright scene. He was a big man, six feet six, genial, and handsome in his blue frock coat, his white neckcloth and broad-brimmed high hat.

Servants came from the kitchen with trays and trays of food, frosty bowls of iced punch, and fine wines for the gentlemen. Soon there wasn't an inch of space left on the large tables under the trees.

"Children, wait now until your elders are served," his father reminded them.

This always seemed unfair to Henry. Grown people, he was sure, never were as hungry as children. But there was comfort in knowing that the supply of good things from the kitchen was endless, and there was more than enough for them all.

Next to the food, the thing Henry liked best about launching parties was the men's conversations. They talked mostly of ships and faraway places they had sailed to, places Henry planned to see someday. He was fascinated by the very sound of them as the men spoke their names—Calcutta, Naples, Cairo, Seville. . . .

Always, sometime before the afternoon was over, their talk turned to the argument about steam.

"Steamships won't ever replace sailing vessels," one man said. "It's just a fad. Wait and see. Ten years from now everybody will have forgotten about steam."

"I'm not so sure," another replied. "Look at the Savannah—crossed to Liverpool in twenty-seven days."

"Yes. But she only used steam for eighty hours of that time—rest of the time she sailed. That proves nothing!"

"Oh, steam is here to stay."

"Humph. Won't stay long after one of the things blows up! And that's just what's going to happen. You'll see!"

Henry always shuddered at that prediction. When he saw a steamship on the river he watched it, fascinated, fearful it might blow up, and yet half hoping it would. Not really hoping, that is. But if one was going to explode, he wanted to see it.

"How about it, Henry," one of the men turned to the boy. "Are you going to build steamships when you grow up and take over the yard?"

"I'm not going to build ships," Henry said: "I'm going to sail in them. All over the world."

The men laughed, and Henry flushed, a little angry with himself for having told of his ambition. He had not told them all of it, however. He was glad they did not know of his plan to write about the things he saw in his travels, and some day to become a famous playwright.

As Henry grew older, his father frequently took him to the shipyard. There Henry saw that the Bergh ships were good ships because only the best of materials and the finest of workmanship went into them. His father would tolerate nothing that was not solid and true.

"Mr. Bergh has hawk-eyes," the carpenters told the boy, "he can tell fifty feet away if a board has been sawed a mite unevenly."

The men admired Christian Bergh, and they liked to work for him. They were proud that the Bergh yard had pioneered in building the first packet boats in New York, and that, right from the start of steam, steamships had been turned out there.

Henry saw that the men respected his father's courage and fairness.

"He's a gentleman and good to his workers," they would say. "But if he thought it was necessary, he could whip any two of us at once. He's not afraid of anything."

Henry knew this was true. There was the time, for example, when Christian Bergh employed Negro workmen in spite of threats from angry mobs. He had calmly answered their threats, saying the color of a man's skin made no difference if he was an honest worker and in need of a job. None of the threats had been carried out.

And how many times the boy had heard, "Your father's the most honest man in New York!" Anyone who knew him could vouch for that.

It was there at the shipyard Henry learned to admire his father's courage, independence, and deep honesty. He hoped he would grow up to be like him.

Though the shipyard was a fascinating place, and Henry was very happy at home, his desire to see the world grew stronger every year. Each time a ship went out, he wished he were on it.

His brother, Christian, Jr., sometimes teased him about it. "You wanted to sail on the Antarctica, Henry, and you know what happened to her!"

Henry knew! She had become lost in the South Seas and put in at a strange island that was swarming with cannibals. Twelve of the crew were killed by the wild men. The rest hid in trees, where they spent a night filled with terror. The tale they told when they got back chilled the blood!

The story was not a pleasant one, but it couldn't shake Henry's wish to travel.

However, Henry took time first to study at Columbia College. Then, after his schooling was finished, for several years he worked in his father's shipyard. It was not until after the yard was sold and Henry received his share of the ample inheritance, that he felt free to go.

When Henry Bergh did sail out of New York Harbor on a bright May morning, bound for Europe, he did not go alone. Sailing with him was his beautiful young wife, Catherine Matilda Taylor.

Matilda was tall and slender, with cream-white skin and dark hair, and wherever she went, people stared at her beauty. Henry was very proud of her.

During the next few years, Henry and Matilda visited France, Spain, England, Greece, Turkey, Egypt, and many other lands. They would come back to the United States for brief visits, and then start out again.

When they were in the States the tall, distinguished-looking gentleman and his charming wife were much in demand socially. In the capitals of Europe they were presented at Court, made friends with royalty and were at home in palaces.

Theirs was a brilliant social life, a life filled

with luxury and ease. And it is doubtful that either of them ever considered it would end.

During their travels, Henry wrote plays as he had planned to do. Some people praised his writing, but many critics did not like it.

Once when a play of his had been harshly criticized, Henry complained to a publisher.

The wise man said, "Oh, don't worry if they say something unpleasant about you or your work. The time to get distressed is when they say **nothing** about you."

Henry Bergh did not know it then, but he was to remember this piece of advice and profit from it.

TWO

GOLD BRAID

When the letter was delivered by special messenger, Matilda knew it was important. She glanced at the clock in the hall, then went to the front window to see if Henry was coming. It was early evening and the New York street was busy with people returning home. But she saw him as he rounded the corner, taller than the rest, hurrying now that he was within sight of their house.

She met him at the door, took his cane and tall silk hat and waited while he opened the letter.

Henry spread it out on the desk and they read it together, both of them a little breathless. The letter announced that Henry Bergh had been appointed Secretary to the American Legation in Russia. It was signed by **Abraham Lincoln, President**.

"It's a great honor, Henry," Matilda spoke first. She was thinking proudly of the qualifications the President had seen in her husband—tact, intelligence, gentility, the special knowledge that comes of being well-traveled, well-read.

"I probably got the appointment because I have a beautiful wife." Henry smiled at Matilda, then looked suddenly concerned. "Are you sure you'll like living in St. Petersburg?"

"Of course I will. But we must start at once getting ready to leave. The letter says we are to sail on June sixth. That's less than four weeks from today!"

This was a different trip from those they had taken for pleasure. London to Paris to Cologne to Berlin—and no time to tarry. Across Poland into Russia.

"It is dangerous to go into Poland at this time," they were told. "The country is in a state of rebellion."

But they had no choice. The trains moved slowly through the country, with Russian soldiers guarding the tracks. A pilot engine preceded them to make sure it was safe. There was no traveling after dark, and when they stopped at night, even the best lodgings were very poor.

Food was scarce. There were not enough candles to light their rooms. There were no sheets on the beds.

"Here in Poland," the innkeeper explained to Matilda, "we are too poor. Those travelers who want sheets must bring their own."

Henry and Matilda were relieved to reach

St. Petersburg and have the long journey at an end.

In Russia, they found there were only three classes of people: the nobility, the military, and the great mass of common people, most of whom were as poor and miserable as the Poles. Because of Henry's position, the Berghs' contacts were chiefly with the nobility.

"As far as I can tell," Henry described his position to Matilda, "my job here seems to be jollying the Czar along in his usual state of good humor."

Never, in all their travels, had they seen anything as lavish as the Russian Court in St. Petersburg. At the glittering Winter Palace they were presented, with great pomp, to the Czar. A few nights later, an even more dazzling ceremony was held for their formal presentation to the Czarina.

"Did you ever see so many jewels?" Matilda whispered to Henry, "Why, Her Majesty **glistens** with diamonds! Isn't it elegant?"

"She looks like a bag of bones, if you ask me," Henry whispered back. Only he had a big voice and the whisper was quite loud.

"Shhhh."

Candlelight gleamed from gold candelabras, striking fire from rubies and diamonds, lighting emeralds and opals, shining on silver hangings and gold brocade and cloth embroidered with pearls. It was rich and brilliant beyond belief.

When the ceremony was finally over and the Berghs were on their way home, Matilda said, "I hear even the toys belonging to the children of the Royal Family are made of gold and studded with precious stones."

"I don't doubt it," Henry said dryly. "By the way, I received a bill myself today for a quantity of gold—gold lace and braid." He chuckled. "For the uniforms of our coachman and footman. In Russia members of the diplomatic corps mustn't ride in carriages with servants who don't dazzle."

But behind the richness and glitter of court life, Henry saw the awful poverty of the masses.

He saw men, women and children—prisoners from the conquered Caucasus Mountains—driven through the streets in chain gangs. When they fell, exhausted and starved, they were prodded by the guards till they stumbled on. Officially, Henry dared not try to help them. And efforts to do so without disclosing his identity failed.

Almost as miserable were the great hordes of common people, living in filth, always hungry and in need. For these too he could offer no help, beyond slipping coins now and then to those whose needs seemed greatest.

One day when Henry and Matilda were out driving, they saw a peasant mercilessly beating a donkey. This was a common sight in Russia. Henry often thought that because the people were so wretched themselves, they had no pity for any living thing.

The donkey was hitched to a cart heavily loaded with wood, and it was clearly impossible for the poor creature to pull it up the hill. Still the peasant stood in the cart, pounding the animal with the club. The donkey brayed in pain, its legs sagged, and under the steady rain of blows it was about to collapse.

Henry ordered the carriage to stop. To Matilda he said, "I can do nothing for the suffering people—but by Jove, if it's possible, I'll save that poor beast's life."

Since he could speak no Russian—in diplomatic circles the official language was French—he asked his footman to come with him and plead with the peasant.

A small crowd had gathered to watch the donkey beater. As Henry and his servant went toward them, the crowd cried out a warning to the man. He dropped the club, jumped off the cart, and stood trembling before them.

There was an explosion of words from the footman, and the poor peasant began to babble, begging, as Henry could tell from his gestures, for

mercy. Then he hastily removed some of the wood from the cart, and in another moment the donkey pulled the lightened cart up the hill. The peasant, picking up the discarded wood, hurried along beside him.

Henry was puzzled. "What did you say to the man?" he asked the footman.

"It was not what I said, Monsieur," the footman answered, "It was this." He touched the gold braid of his uniform.

"People here are frightened of uniforms," he explained. "Men in uniforms have been cruel to them. You can accomplish much in Russia with a few yards of gold braid."

Henry laughed heartily. "At last," he cried, "I've found a use for gold braid!"

Beginning that day, Henry and the footman made themselves a committee of two for the prevention of cruelty to animals in St. Petersburg. They drove through the streets, watching for cases of brutality. Each time they found one, the footman's appearance brought the same results. Henry often wondered what his servant said when he flung the cascade of angry words at the culprits. He hoped the language was clean. He never found out. At any rate, the gold braid always worked like magic!

Henry and Matilda found life in Russia varied

and interesting. But as their second winter there approached, each of them worried for fear the other's health would be hurt by the long months of bitter cold that lay ahead.

The year before, the first snow had fallen on September 29th. On May 25th, Henry recorded in his diary, "There is still snow!" Eight months of winter, and most of it intensely cold.

"Would you like to try and get a diplomatic appointment in some other country?" Matilda asked him.

"No," said Henry slowly. "As a matter of fact, I'm tired of dealing with stupid politicians and vain monarchs. Besides, I have something else in mind.

"Writing?"

He smiled. "I played with that long enough. It was fun, and I had to do it. But I will never be a **great** writer, Matilda. No, it's this. In every country we know—including our own United States--we've been sickened by the amount of cruelty to animals we've seen. Somehow, I'd never thought of doing anything about it before. But this past year, I've seen how much could be accomplished here in Russia with a little assumed authority and some tinsel braid. Think what could be done in the United States, with **real** authority, an organization with legal powers behind it!" Then he told her of the organization in England—The Royal

Society for the Prevention of Cruelty to Animals—
which was working well there.

"I would like to resign here, and stop in London
on our way home. I want to talk to Lord Harrowby
who founded the English Society," he said. "I want to
stay long enough to study the organization thoroughly,
see how it works, find out its problems and how they
are being met. Are you willing to do this, Matilda?"

"Of course I am, Henry," Matilda agreed. "But
I'm afraid this is a tremendous task you have chosen
for yourself. It will be very hard, especially at this
time, with the states still at war and the country
divided and uncertain."

"Yes, I know that," Henry said. "It will be
difficult to interest people in animals when human
suffering is so great. I don't expect it to be easy."

"There will be ridicule you must be prepared for,
and battles with the enemies you are bound to make."

"That is true," Henry answered. "When you tell
a man how to treat his animals, you are meddling with
what he considers his own private property. Men are
all dependent—either directly or indirectly—on
animals for their daily needs. And yet a man who owns
a beast feels he has a right to neglect it, mistreat it,
even torture it, simply because it is **his**. That isn't
right."

Matilda, too, knew it wasn't right. She did not want to discourage Henry, but she did caution him with warnings.

That fall, before the severest weather set in, the Berghs left for England. Henry spent months there studying the Royal Society for the Prevention of Cruelty to Animals. He made notes, talked to many people, formed plans. The idea took shape and grew. With its growth, his enthusiasm increased. He was anxious to get back to the States and start work, but first he wanted to learn all he could.

The Berghs were still in England when they received the joyous news that the Civil War in the United States was over.

Then, a few weeks later, came the tragic message that Abraham Lincoln had been assassinated. Henry Bergh had keenly admired Lincoln, and he was shocked and saddened by the President's death. He and Matilda knelt in St. James's Hall at the memorial service held for Lincoln, and Henry knew they were going back to a country where everything would be more difficult because it had lost its leader.

The Berghs sailed for New York on the afternoon of June 13, 1865, headed for trouble and years of hard work.

THREE

"YOU CAN'T DO THAT ANY MORE!"

"There!" said Matilda as she pressed the postage stamp firmly. "That's the last one. Now all we have to do is mail them and wait for the answers."

For several days she and Henry had been writing letters. It was Henry's first step in founding the new society. The letters, sent to people all over New York, explained the purpose of the organization and asked for their help.

Next Henry drew up a paper which he took to the most prominent citizens in New York and asked them to sign.

The paper read:

PATRONS
of a Society Proposed to be Founded
for the Prevention of Cruelty to Dumb Animals.

The undersigned, sensible of the cruelties inflicted

upon dumb animals by thoughtless and inhuman persons, and desirous of suppressing same—alike from considerations affecting the well-being of society as well as mercy to the brute creations—consent to become patrons of a Society having in the view realization of these objects.

Some of the people were angered by Henry's plea. From these he received sharp replies. "You are meddling in something that is none of your business," many of them wrote.

Or, refusing to sign the paper, men would say, "It's a ridiculous idea, Bergh. If you take my advice, you'll forget the whole thing."

Henry knew some of these men were afraid of it. Those who were making money out of the street railways with their horse-drawn cars, those who controlled the great stock yards, railroad men who got wealthy through the sale of cattle—none of these wanted anyone interfering with the way they treated animals. Henry sensed at once that such men would be among his most powerful enemies.

Others ignored Henry's plea. Many of these were too busy building fortunes to worry about cruelties to dogs and horses! The West, with its vast riches, was opening up rapidly. Men were scheming how to grab land, gold, oil, coal, how to control grain markets, fur markets and the ever-spreading railroads. Their answer to Henry, if they heard him at all, was, "I have more important things to do."

Some thought he was crazy. And some, who he had been sure would help, scoffed. A clergyman, for example, said impatiently, "Bah! This is no time for sentiment," and dismissed it.

Henry tried, always, to make such people understand that his motive was not a sentimental one. It was a matter of common sense, and of right and wrong.

"Without animals," he would say to them, "you would have no meat, no milk, no eggs. There would be fewer vegetables and little grain, because the farmer would have to pull his own plow. You would have to walk everywhere you go instead of riding. Your shoes, your coat, that beaver hat, your gloves, the silk scarf you are wearing—all of these things and many more you have only because of the world's dumb creatures. Since we are so dependent on them, I consider it morally wrong to be needlessly cruel to them. In addition, it is wasteful. Badly treated animals can't work as well as those that have known kindness and care."

There were some men in the city, of course, who agreed with Henry and signed the paper. Among them

31

were many prominent names—Frank Leslie, whose magazine was to help Bergh fight his battles, Peter Cooper, James Roosevelt, John Jacob Astor, Horace Greeley, and many others.

There were seventy names signed to the paper when Henry decided it was time to call a meeting and make plans for a charter and laws. He had been working on his idea then for seven months.

The meeting was held on February 8, 1866. It was a very stormy night, and Henry pulled up the fur collar of his overcoat as he faced the wind. The streets were almost deserted, and he wondered gloomily if anybody but himself would come out in such weather.

When the meeting was called to order, twenty-five men were there. The hall was cold, and everyone was wet and uncomfortable. It was hard to feel very enthusiastic about anything. Henry made a brief speech, and a committee of three was elected to draw up a charter for the proposed society. Henry promised, when the charter was ready, to take it to Albany and place it before the State Legislature. Until the State granted them a charter, and then passed an anti-cruelty law, the real work could not begin.

The weeks Henry spent storming Albany were hard ones. He talked until his voice was ragged—arguing with senators, reasoning with politicians,

Paul Brown '41

speaking before committees, trying to win them over to the cause in which he believed so firmly. In New York he had a small but influential group of men behind him.

Finally, on April 19th, the bill chartering the Society was passed. Nine days later the Anti-Cruelty Law went through, and Bergh's work in Albany was finished. He was pleased with both documents.

The charter not only provided for the forming of the American Society for the Prevention of Cruelty to Animals, but it stated that the police must help the Society's agents enforce the law, and that half the fines collected should be given to the Society.

The law said that any person who should "By his act or neglect, maliciously kill, maim, wound, injure, torture or cruelly beat any horse, mule, ox, cattle, sheep or other animal belonging to himself or another" should be judged guilty of a misdemeanor.

Furthermore, it made it a misdemeanor for a person to turn loose an old or disabled mule or horse in the streets for more than three hours. Henry was glad this law was passed. He had always been outraged by the number of old horses abandoned to starve and die in the streets because their owners found this the easiest way to get rid of them. He came back to New York feeling triumphant, with a copy of the bill and the charter in his pocket.

He was hurrying home from the railroad station when he stopped short at the sight of a man beating his horse. Bergh walked up to the man and said politely, "My friend, you can't do that any more."

The man stared at him in amazement. "Can't beat my own horse?" he asked. "The devil I can't!" He raised the heavy whip and began again to lash the poor animal.

Henry put a restraining hand on his arm and said, "You are not aware, perhaps, but you are breaking the law. I can have you arrested for that." He reached into his pocket for the copy of the law.

The fellow jumped off the wagon, and turned his attention from the horse to Bergh. "You're crazy!" he shouted, "Get along—you're mad." He flourished the whip threateningly at Bergh.

Henry didn't budge. "I'm not crazy—I'm warning you that you risk arrest."

The man glowered at Henry. "Listen. If you wanna fight—come on. I'll fight you."

Henry wanted to. But he didn't think it was a very dignified way of handling his first case. Before he could answer, the horse started up, and the fellow jumped onto the wagon and was off, shaking his fist at Henry and calling him names.

Henry didn't feel quite as jaunty as he had before. When he reached home he said to Matilda, "Enforcing the law here in America where everyone is independent is going to be very different from enforcing it in Russia where people are frightened by a little gold braid."

A few days after his return, the new Society had its first meeting. On this warm spring night, April 23, 1866, there at Clinton Hall, it was a very different meeting from the one held in February. A good crowd gathered, and there were enthusiastic speeches and plans for the future. People offered money—some as much as a thousand dollars —to help support the new Society. They elected Henry Bergh president.

The next morning Henry went down to the modest headquarters that he had rented for the new society and began work. The building was a plain one on Broadway at the corner of Twelfth Street. The office was one small work room and a tiny reception hall. It was simply furnished: five plain kitchen chairs, a desk, a cheap matting on the floor.

Henry made his first arrest when he saw a butcher driving a cart load of calves down the street. It was a common sight, and one that had always angered Bergh. The calves' legs were tied, and the poor creatures were thrown into the cart helter-skelter, one on top of another. As the cart rumbled over the cobble-stones, the helpless animals gouged one another with their sharp hooves, their heads bumped until they bled, and their bellowings could be heard long before the cart was in sight.

Henry yelled at the butcher to stop. But he only whipped his horses and made them go faster. Henry was determined to see this case to a finish. He ran after the wagon, block after block, from Broadway to the East River, and finally caught up with it when it had to stop at the Williamsburg Ferry.

"Yah—you're crazy," the butcher yelled when he was told he must untie the calves and stand them up in the cart or he would be arrested. Henry tried to reason with the fellow, but it did no good.

So, he carried out his threat to arrest him.

In court the magistrate knew nothing of Bergh's American Society for the Prevention of Cruelty to Animals. Hadn't people always carted calves and sheep in that manner?

"They always have, Your Honor, but they can't any longer," Henry said. "It is cruelty, and here is the law."

The magistrate was afraid to convict the butcher. How other judges would laugh if they found he had sent a man to jail on such a silly charge!

*Old horses used to be turned out into the streets
to starve and die.*

However, he fined the fellow a small amount and let him go.

During the next few weeks, Bergh saw case after case either dismissed or the culprit made only to pay a small fine. He knew now it would take much time and labor to make the Society function. "I have the law," he said. "But **how** can I enforce it?"

Before the American Society for the Prevention of Cruelty to Animals was a month old, he and Matilda realized their big problem was that most people did not know about the Society, and many of those who did know were indifferent. Men laughed when Henry tried to arrest them. The judges winked when the cases were presented.

"We must do something so that everybody in the city will know about the Society," Henry went over the problem with Matilda. "People must be stirred up. They must talk about it, read about it, argue about it—then the indifference will cease. These small cases have only caused a trickle of interest. We need a splash."

Henry lay awake nights trying to figure out what to do.

Then one warm May evening, after a whole day of pounding the streets, he came home smiling. "Matilda! I have it, " he said. "Turtles!"

FOUR

THE CASE OF THE FORTY TURTLES

Early the next morning, Henry and two police-men walked down to the waterfront.

He had seen the turtles the afternoon before on the deck of a schooner. There were 40 live green turtles brought up from the tropics. They lay on their backs, their fins pierced and tied with thongs so they could not move. Henry questioned a member of the crew. The man admitted they had been like that for several weeks without food or water.

Bergh felt sorry for the poor creatures. But more than that, he saw here in the lowly turtle a means of stirring up the indifferent public. Most people would think a turtle's suffering unworthy of consideration. If he came to their defense, it was probable that before long most of the city would know about it.

Henry and the policemen boarded the schooner and, pointing to the pile of turtles, Henry said, "This is clearly a case of cruelty, officers. I demand the arrest of Captain Nehemiah Calhoun and his entire crew."

The Captain was outraged. The men swore and bellowed. But the policemen and Bergh marched them off the ship and toward the station house.

What a parade they made! The rough sailors in their dirty, fishy clothes; the Captain cursing and fuming; the policemen hurrying them on; and Henry, immaculately dressed, tall and dignified, at the head of the procession.

A rag-tag string of children hooted and howled as they followed. People leaned out windows and hurried to the doorways to watch. The parade grew as it went along. By the time they reached the station house, it was a near riot!

Several days later, when the trial opened, the courtroom was packed. People came from all over the city to see a man crazy enough to defend a boat load of turtles.

The Society had no money to spend on a lawyer so Henry argued his own case. He was not a lawyer, but he had received a written permit to act as counsel for the ASPCA. The permit was signed by the County District Attorney and the State Attorney General.

The Captain of the schooner had hired a clever lawyer named Anderson to defend him and his crew.

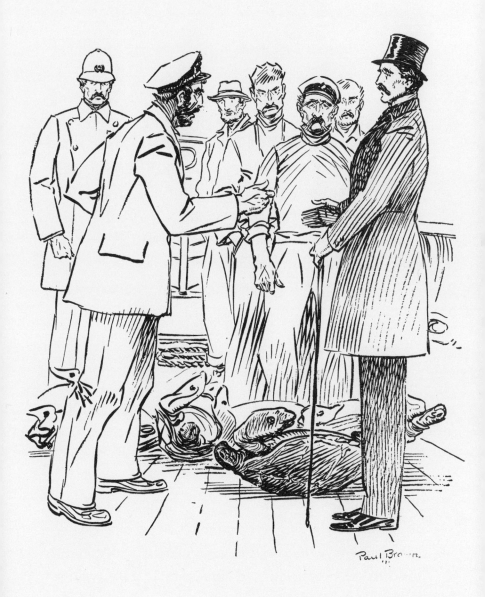

Anderson was an experienced trial lawyer, and Henry knew it would be a battle.

Anderson started off by saying that the turtle was not an animal, and that since the law applied only to cruelty to animals, Bergh had no case against the men.

At these words the crowd clapped and cheered. "He's got the old turtle lover there!" a boy shouted, and everyone roared. The judge rapped for order.

Henry said, "If it is not an animal, Mr. Anderson, what is it? There are three kingdoms in nature: animal, vegetable, and mineral. Surely the turtle cannot be called a vegetable, nor a mineral."

There was a moment of silence, and Henry went on, "The turtle may be **low** in the animal species, but it can feel. It suffers with pain."

Anderson glared at Bergh and then asked, "Do you think it is more cruel to place a turtle on his back and tie his fins than to leave him lying in his natural position during a voyage?"

"Undoubtedly," Bergh said quietly. "It is always cruel to reverse the order of nature."

The lawyer was a little angered by Henry's quick and neat answers. He said sarcastically, "But wasn't it cruel then, Mr. Bergh, to take the turtles out of the water at all. Did nature intend that?"

The crowd cheered again, and someone yelled,

"Give Bergh a plate of turtle soup. He needs it."

Again the judge ordered silence. Henry smiled at his opponent and said, "I see, Mr. Anderson, you know little about turtles. Turtles are amphibians. The turtle comes out of the water to lay its eggs and watch the hatching of its young. It lives both on land and in the water."

Anderson had no answer to make to this. But hour after hour the arguing went on. When the court closed for the day, Henry saw that the case would not end in a hurry.

The next morning the whole town was talking! The newspapers printed stories about the trial. Some of them made fun of Bergh. One published a cartoon of Bergh and a big turtle. The turtle was hugging him with its flippers and saying, "You're the only friend in the world that loves me living!"

When Henry walked to the courthouse that day he noticed a crowd laughing at something in the window of a nearby restaurant. Henry went over to look. He saw a large turtle lying on a bed of soft yellow corn silk, a pillow under its head. Above the creature was a placard which read:

"Having no desire to wound the feelings of any member of the American Society for the

Prevention of Cruelty to Animals, or of its President, Henry Bergh, we have done what we could for the comfort of this poor turtle during the few remaining days of his life. He will be served in soups and steaks on Thursday and Friday. Members of the aforesaid Society and others are invited to come and do justice to his memory."

Henry's eyes twinkled as he read it. And he wasn't disturbed at all when people in the crowd rudely pointed at him and said, "There's Bergh. . . . There's the turtle man." He looked quietly past them, his head high, his face calm. The words of the London publisher came back to Henry now—"The time to get distressed is when they say **nothing** about you."

For six weeks the case was talked of, argued about, written up in papers and magazines.

On July 10th the judge finally gave his decision. Henry lost. The judge said, "A turtle is an insect, not an animal. . . . To bore holes in a turtle's fin does not hurt him more than the bite of a mosquito hurts a human."

Henry knew it was not only ridiculous but incorrect to call a turtle an insect! It was a stupid decision in every respect. He wrote to the great naturalist Agassiz and asked his opinion. Agassiz agreed that the treatment of the turtles was cruelty to animals. He wrote a letter to Bergh: "To say that the turtle does not suffer when dragged from its natural haunts and tied so it cannot move is absurd." He said, too, that if a turtle was forced to stay on its back for a length of time, it died from the pain and unaccustomed pressure.

Agassiz surely should know turtles! In order to study them, he had lived with them—tubs full of little soft-shelled turtles all around the house, a huge Galapagos tortoise in his front hall, terrapins under the stairs, and even a couple of ferocious snappers behind bars in a big box.

But the words of the naturalists and all of Henry's arguments could not change the judge's decision.

Even though he had lost the case, Henry had won his point. People were no longer indifferent to the ASPCA. Everybody knew about it, and its founder, Henry Bergh, was rapidly becoming well-known.

The turtle case was a turning point in Henry's life and in the success of the Society. They were in the spotlight now!

Bergh's work increased by leaps and bounds. People began reporting cases to him: sick horses forced to work, brutalities of dog and cock fights, abandoned cattle, the beating of horses, dogs, cats, cruelties of all kinds.

Even if Henry worked twenty-four hours a day, he could not do all that needed to be done. So, after a few months, agents were hired at sixteen dollars a week to help him with investigations and arrests. Anxiously Henry watched the expenses of the Society mount—there was rent to pay, the fuel bill to meet, postage and office supplies to buy.

He came to Matilda one day, troubled. "Unless we have money—a good deal of money—the Society can't go on."

"We have property we could give to the Society and save it, Henry."

This was what Henry wanted to hear. He looked down at her affectionately. "I did not wish to ask you to make financial sacrifices for the Society," he said. "You have already given up a great deal—time, our social life, even friends who have dropped us because of all the ridicule. . . ."

"No matter. They could not have been true friends," she said. Then she smiled at him and said, "Besides, we've started something, Henry. Something big. And nothing can make us give up now!"

FIVE

FRIENDS AND ENEMIES

"I wish you didn't need to go out in this storm," Matilda said anxiously.

The room glowed with warmth and light, and as Henry rose from his chair by the fire he said, "So do I. It's far more pleasant here!"

Outdoors sleet fell, crusting the snow. Dark had come early with the storm. People walked slowly and stiff-legged, fearful of falling, bent with the wind.

Henry pulled on a long, heavy coat, and thrust his feet into high boots.

"The worse the weather, the heavier the work," he commented. "I'm going up to the Drove Yard first. Remember the last time I went up there on a night like this, Matilda? Hundreds of head of cattle crowded in the open yard, each of them coated with a sheet of ice. It will be the same tonight, I'll bet. But if I arrest the fellows often enough, they **will** build barns."

Matilda watched from the window, but Henry was

out of sight in the storm almost at once. She worried about him because he had so little rest. She knew that when he did come home, no matter how late the hour, there would still be work for him to do: letters to answer, articles to write, a speech to prepare.

He was asked often now to lecture about his work. Usually he talked to grown-ups, but sometimes he spoke to great gatherings of children. He was always pleased when invited to talk before children, for he considered them very important in the campaign against cruelty.

He was busy, too, helping groups outside New York City organize societies similar to the ASPCA.

Regardless of when he went to bed, he was up before dawn. With the first light of day he started for the railroad yards to check on the unloading of cattle cars. From then on, hour after hour, he tirelessly made his rounds.

Henry had become a familiar figure around New York—a feared but respected one.

People on overloaded horse-drawn street cars groaned at the sight of him. "Here comes Bergh!"

"Men and boys off," he would command, stopping the car. When he considered it light enough so the poor horses could pull it without straining to death, he would wave it on. Wives yelled messages to their husbands who were left behind; girls went home without their escorts; people fumed and fussed, but they always obeyed.

The strength of the tall, aristocratic gentleman was often a surprise. Once when a man refused to get off, Bergh picked him up by the nape of the neck and neatly set him down on the curb.

There was the time two butchers with a cart load of calves refused to untie the animals and stand them up in the dray. "It don't hurt'em none," they yelled at Bergh. "Mind yer own business."

Henry snatched them off the wagon and bumped their heads smartly together. "You see, it does hurt. Doesn't it?" he said to the yowling men. "Now will you do as I say, or must I arrest you?"

The men obeyed speedily.

Whether a man was poor or wealthy made no difference to Bergh. All must obey the law. One sunny spring day he made half the society people in New York City angry by walking through Central Park and down fashionable Fifth Avenue carrying a bushel basket and collecting bit burrs.

Bit burrs were circular pieces of leather, one side of which was studded with tacks or sharp bristles. The burr was fastened to the bit that went into the horse's mouth, and as it tore into the tender flesh of the cheeks, the animal reared its head in pain, pranced and looked very spirited. People considered it stylish to have prancing, frisky horses drawing their carriages. The vanity of the owners was satisfied, but none of the drivers gave a thought to the horses.

Henry made them think. As he stopped each carriage and removed the burrs, he handed out court summonses, and with each summons he delivered a scorching lecture. He had a big voice, and it was natural for a crowd to gather. There were many carriage owners with red faces on Fifth Avenue that day, but their horses were more comfortable.

No problem was too large for him to tackle, no suffering too small for him to notice. Once he saw a cow and calf being driven through the streets, the little calf bellowing with hunger. The mother wanted to feed him, and mooed pitifully, but the driver kept them apart with a long stick. Henry stopped him and made him let the calf feed right there on the city street. People tarried, curious to watch the calf have its dinner, and Henry stood by until he was sure the animal had had enough.

Bergh's bold demands, his power, both angered and amazed people.

Once, going past a new building, he heard the faint but distressed mewing of a cat. Henry began to hunt for it. He was horrified to learn that workmen had cruelly imprisoned the animal in the wall. The cat had

crawled into a space in a girder and been sealed in.

"You will have to tear open this wall," Henry told the builder firmly, "and release the animal."

The man begged, pleaded, threatened, and almost wept as he told Bergh how much money it would cost him. But the wall came down, and the cat, skinny and scared, was rescued.

As Bergh's work grew heavier, the papers heaped more and more ridicule on him. Not all the papers, however. Horace Greeley's New York Tribune regularly printed editorials and stories in his favor. Frank Leslie's Illustrated Weekly had backed him and the ASPCA from the start.

But others, notably James Gordon Bennett's powerful New York Herald, poked fun at him continually and unmercifully.

Henry was an extremely sensitive person, and always proud and careful of his appearance. It hurt him when people were amused at a picture of him with donkey ears, surrounded by animals laughing at him, or a caricature of him wearing a horse blanket instead of a coat.

When he forced the driver of an overloaded wagon to get off and walk, a cartoon was published of a horse riding in a cart pulled by a man. Underneath was printed, "Cruelty to Animals—How the Thing Is

Reversed in the New Regime."

His enemies printed articles accusing him of wanting to harbor bugs and fleas and saying he was worse than the ancient Egyptians who worshiped crocodiles.

One magazine sarcastically suggested that human beings should band together and protect themselves against Bergh by forming a Society for the Prevention of Cruelty Toward Men by Animals. A Sunday paper was unjust enough to say Bergh was living off money that other people had donated to the Society.

Though he pretended to pay no attention to these, Matilda knew that it hurt him to be so misunderstood and ridiculed.

People in all walks of life took sides for or against Bergh. Among his friends were poor people and rich people and people he did not know. Children came into the office with pennies to help support his work. A shabbily dressed woman handed Bergh an envelope and hurried away before he opened it. It contained fifty dollars for the ASPCA.

Strong in his support, right from the start, was the theater world. One of the first gifts to the Society was a hundred dollars from the great actor Edwin Booth. This pleased Bergh, who always loved the theater, and never, unless his work was very heavy, missed the opening of a new play.

A brilliant young lawyer, Elbridge T. Gerry, became interested in the Society and offered to serve as its counsel so Henry could be relieved of the court work. His backers included Mayor Hoffman of New York City and other men prominent politically and socially, as well as teamsters, stable-hands, and shopkeepers. The work knew no social boundaries.

His enemies, too, were numbered among all kinds and classes of people. Men who grew wealthy by encouraging the overloading of horse-cars hated him. The rag-pickers who forced hungry dogs to draw their carts feared him. There were scheming dairymen who were his enemies because he investigated their dirty, crowded stables and arrested them for milking sick cows. Moneyed sportsmen—led by the publisher James Gordon Bennett—attacked him because he was against their fashionable "pigeon shoots" where thousands of birds were shot for fun, the injured allowed to die lingering deaths. Men of the New York underworld fought him because he tried to outlaw their cruel dogfights and cockfights.

There were threats against his life. These frightened Matilda, but Henry took them calmly.

One would-be assassin was bold enough to tell Henry he would call at his house on a certain night before midnight to kill him. Henry sat down in the living room to wait. As the clock ticked on, Matilda became more and more nervous.

"You should have gone somewhere—some place where you could have been protected," she cried, "you're in danger here!"

Henry looked up from the book he was reading. "Barking dogs seldom bite," he said comfortingly, "and scoundrels who threaten never shoot."

They waited until after midnight, and nobody came.

"Drat the fellow!" Henry yawned as they started for bed. "It's been a nuisance staying up till this hour when I have so much to do tomorrow."

In spite of the threats he was never afraid. He went into the toughest neighborhoods, the darkest places, any time of the day or night when there was work to be done there.

SIX

THE DOG FIGHT KING

Of all the tough streets in New York City in the 1860s, the toughest by far was Water Street. The big homes and wide lawns that had been there when Henry was a child had disappeared with the rapid growth of the city. Now the street was lined with cheap dance halls, sailors' boardinghouses, gambling dives, and saloons.

On Water Street, too, was Kit Burn's infamous establishment. Kit was the Dog Fight King of New York, and many people considered him and his place one of the worst influences in the city.

"Please do something about Kit Burn," Henry heard hundreds of times. "It is certainly cruelty to animals to throw dogs into a pit and force them to kill one another. . . . Kit's place is a shame to the city . . . the dogfights are degrading."

Henry knew all these things were true. But Kit was a slippery customer. He was hard to catch.

From the front, his place looked like any other Water Street saloon: a line of rough, sweaty men at the bar, flyspecked pictures of prize fighters on the walls, gamblers arguing over cards in the back room.

Behind this front, however, Kit Burn's place was different from the others. A door in the back room opened into a narrow, winding passage that led to the cellar. As one descended into the cellar, he first heard the sound of the dogs, barking and whining, dragging at chains. Then he saw them in the dim light, each chained to a small stall, living in the dank, foul-smelling half-dark until Kit chose to haul them upstairs to kill or be killed.

These were not Kit's prize dogs. These were second-raters, used in preliminary fights.

The choice dogs were kept above the saloon in a room on the second floor reached by a back stairs. Here Kit trained fighters whose names were famous in New York's underworld: Belcher, the white bull terrier that killed seven dogs before he was finished off. Hunky, on whom fortunes had been staked. Jack the Ratter, and many others.

The very method of training the dogs for fighting was cruel. They were put on a revolving table know as "The Wheel." Then strange dogs were brought in and chained near them, and the dog on the table was goaded to fight. While the trainer held the angry dog, the animal ran. But he simply went around in circles on the turntable, never getting any nearer his chained enemy, his speed increasing with his fury. This would be kept up for two hours or more, often until the dog dropped from exhaustion. After this, the poor animal was carried to a tub of lukewarm water, then thrown into a tub of cold water. If this did not revive him, the trainer rubbed him down with alcohol.

Such training not only kept the dogs slim and tough, but it also increased their endurance and made them ferocious. Kit had no pity for the dogs. If one died from this harsh treatment, he said, "Good riddance. He would have lost me money in the pit anyhow, the weakling."

The hall where the fights were held was behind the barroom. Seats were arranged in stadium fashion, from the floor to the ceiling. Into this hall crowded gamblers, bums, crooked ward politicians, the scum of New York's underworld.

In the center of the room was the pit, seventeen feet long, and about half that wide, oval-shaped. In this pit the snarling dogs were set on one another by their owners. While they fought, the men cheered and cursed, yelled and stomped, until one of the dogs killed the other or injured it so badly it could no longer stand. Then bets were paid off and the pit was cleared for the next fight.

None of the men had any feeling for the animals. The injured dog was usually thrown aside, uncared-for, no matter how courageously he had fought. He was forgotten in a moment except by those who were angry at him because his losing the fight had cost them money.

Henry Bergh wanted very much to have Kit Burn arrested and put a stop to this ugly business. But in order to arrest Kit, he had to catch him during a fight, with the dogs as evidence.

Now Kit was not a bright person. A stout man with a red pockmarked face and scrubby beard, he looked rather stupid. But he had one talent. He could recognize an ASPCA agent a block away. Bergh, of course, he knew. It was impossible for Henry to get into one of his fights. But even when Henry's aides, dressed as waterfront bums, tried to get in, Kit sensed who they were. He could not be fooled.

One day when Bergh was walking by Burn's place, he saw something he had never noticed before. The building was two stories high in front, one story in back. And on the rear roof was a skylight. Since it was in the center of the roof, it might be just above the pit. With the weather warm for mid-April, the window probably would be open.

It was easy for Henry to learn when a dogfight was to be held. Kit was so brazen he actually advertised the events with posters.

So, a few nights later Henry and a policeman crept through the shadows toward Kit's place. They came the back way and approached the hall slowly, and Henry was grateful for the din. As quietly as possible they climbed up the wall, onto the roof.

The skylight was open, and, as Henry hoped, it was right above the pit. They waited until Kit and a fellow named Barry, each with a dog in his arms, climbed into the pit.

Then they jumped!

The hall was a bedlam! Men pushed each other in the rush to get out, yelling, "Beat it, de cops. . . . Dere's Bergh. . . . Lemme outa here. . . ." Dogs chained under seats yelped and barked. Kit Burn's curses blasted the air. In a few minutes everybody on Water Street had turned out to see Bergh and the policeman march Kit and Barry, with their prize dogs, to the station house. Burn's arrest was a big event on the Lower East Side. The same judge that Henry had argued before in the turtle case tried Kit and Barry. Once again he decided against Bergh.

The judge dismissed the fellows on the grounds that even though Henry had seen the dogs and the men in the pit it proved nothing because he had not seen Kit nor Barry actually goad the dogs to fight!

This decision was a blow to Henry. He said angrily to Matilda, "I'll get that Kit Burn yet—and with evidence **no** judge can ignore. I'll get him if it takes ten years."

When Kit Burn swaggered out of the courtroom and went back to his establishment, he looked very cocky. He strutted down Water Street, inviting congratulations. At his saloon he handed out free drinks in a grand manner, and waved people in from the street to help him celebrate.

Actually, however, Kit didn't feel so happy. In the first place, all the men who were at the fight the night Bergh broke it up demanded their admission money back. This cost Kit eight hundred dollars.

In the second place, he was scared now of future raids. The story of his arrest had appeared in all the papers. People were writing in to the police demanding to know why such a demoralizing business as Kit's was allowed to exist.

Now, instead of advertising his fights, he had to keep them secret. This made it difficult to get a crowd. Business dropped, and with it dropped Kit's spirits.

In the meantime, Henry was busy raiding smaller cock and dogfight establishments. With every raid, Kit's nervousness increased.

Finally, a year after his arrest, Kit announced that he was going to give up his place and go away. Ironically, he rented the hall to a preacher who held prayer meetings and hymn sings there. Kit thought this was a good joke. He went to Philadelphia, "to retire," so he said.

Henry knew better. "He'll be back," he told Matilda. "You'll see. I'll get him next time."

Kit came back before the year was out and reopened his place.

This time Henry planned his raid very carefully. It was a frosty November night, and most Water Street people were indoors. Henry demanded a large number of policemen to help him—enough so Kit's place was completely surrounded. The police had assembled so quietly, no one in the hall suspected their presence.

When Henry gave the signal, they rushed the place. They poured in to find two dogs in the pit fighting fiercely, Kit urging one of them on, his opponent goading the other. It happened so fast, the men did not know what was going on until they saw the swarms of policemen.

Their warnings, "Douse de glim. . . . Run, de cops . . . ," came too late. Every possible exit was guarded, and no one escaped. Every man in the hall was arrested, and all dogs were taken as evidence.

There was nothing swaggering about Kit now. A coward, he was completely broken as he waited trial. At the mere mention of imprisonment he wept. He was scared, because he knew he had been caught red-handed this time. He whimpered and moaned and complained again and again that his renting the place to the preacher had ruined him.

"Every once in a while he'd say a prayer for me," he lamented. "And it took my luck away."

Kit was not to go to jail, however. He died before his case was tried. His death did not soften Bergh's contempt for him. That night Henry wrote in his diary, "On today, the 18th of December, Kit Burn died at his place in Water Street, thus ridding the city of one of its worst pests."

After Kit was gone, Henry doubled his efforts against the smaller dogfight establishments. He wanted to run them out before another ringleader tried to take Burn's place.

It was a common sight now for Henry's small office to be crowded with confiscated dogs and crowing roosters. Milling about outside were their angry owners, demanding their birds and animals back, threatening Henry.

"Gimmee my birds, you crook. Whattya doin'? Fattening 'em up to eat, that's what, you old thief, Dat dog cost me money. You ain't got no right to keep him ."

But Henry paid no attention. He went steadily on, planning his raids. In this campaign, for the first time, Bergh had practically everybody on his side. All the newspapers backed him, and men who fought him on all other issues supported him in this. With public opinion so strong, he had the courts and the entire police force behind him.

Now the fights were held in the greatest secrecy. The term "dog fight" was not even used any more—the promoters called them "shake-ups." News of a coming "shake-up" was spread, not by words, but by signals and codes.

In spite of all this stealth, it became almost impossible to hold a fight without having it raided. Such a business was profitless and dangerous, and before long the last of the establishments closed its doors.

Many of the promoters turned to other businesses, but some, it was known, had moved out onto Long Island where fights were held hidden in the woods. Sooner or later these, too, would have to be found out.

But in the meantime, Henry had other things to do. And there were new threats and more trouble ahead.

SEVEN

TROUBLE IN ALBANY

For weeks Henry had been spending every spare moment at a drawing board. When Matilda asked him what he was doing, his eyes twinkled and he said, "Wait until I finish, and I'll tell you."

One day he brought her the completed drawing. She looked at it, puzzled, and said, "It's a strange kind of wagon. . . . "

"It's a design for a horse ambulance," Henry said proudly. "I'm going to take this to a good wagonmaker and have one built. With a conveyance of this kind we will be able to save the lives of hundreds of horses a year."

Rescuing horses that had fallen was a problem Henry had long wanted to solve. In winter, they often slipped on the ice and were unable to get up even though their injuries might be slight. There they were left to freeze or take a fatal cold, or perhaps break a leg in their frantic efforts to rise. Moved to a stable, many would have lived.

In the summer they keeled over from sunstroke and heat prostration, and there on the hot streets little could be done to save them.

The year round horses fell, struck by a sudden and temporary paralysis—the result of their having been left in a stall too long. These were usually needlessly destroyed because it was not possible to get them to a shelter for care.

"I think the ambulance is a wonderful idea," Matilda said, studying the drawing, "but won't it be expensive to build?"

"Yes, I'm afraid so," Henry said. "Six or seven hundred dollars, possibly more. But when you consider the price of a good horse, the ambulance, I am sure, will pay for itself in a very short time." He frowned. "I'll have to raise the money for it myself. And find some place where we can keep it, since we have no stable."

Matilda saw the look of distaste on Henry's face at this suggestion. She knew that the hardest part of her husband's job was asking people for donations. He hated it.

However, Henry was able in a short while to raise the money for the ambulance, and a wagonmaker went right to work on it. It was hard to build, because nothing like it had ever been made before. But one hot day in mid-July, Henry came home to tell Matilda it was finished. His worry about where to keep the ambulance had been solved, too. The city would let him store it and stable its team of horses in an empty firehouse.

This was the first ambulance of any kind New York had ever seen, and it was an immediate success! Some people, of course, criticized it, saying: "We don't even have such a thing for human beings! A horse ambulance indeed! Why should animals be so pampered?"

But most people thought it was both beneficial and elegant. It never moved but a crowd followed. Once the curtain at Wallach's Theater was late because the ambulance passed just as the show was ready to start. People going into the theater stopped to look, many of them trailing it for a block or so.

The ambulance was painted a shiny red, with the ASPCA's name printed in fancy gold letters. It had a bottom that could be drawn out, forming a sloping platform on which the injured horse was placed. Then gently, by the use of a rope and a windlass, the animal was drawn into the wagon.

It carried a sling to support the horse if its legs were injured, and a well-equipped first-aid kit, and it

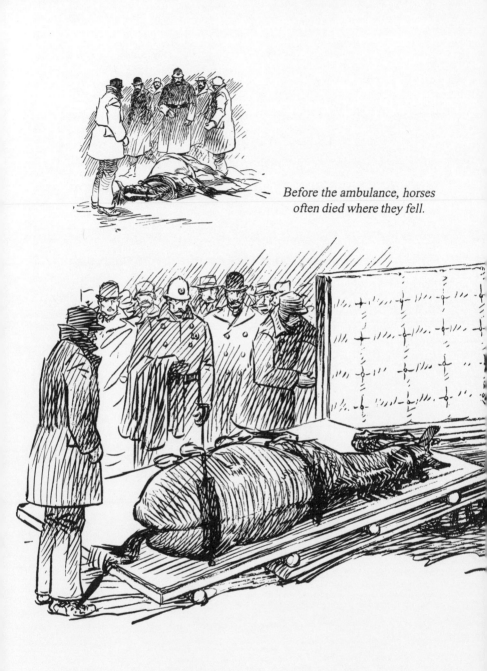

Before the ambulance, horses often died where they fell.

had fine springs and rubber pads to make transportation comfortable.

Henry was very pleased with the ambulance's success. It proved useful not only for horses, but for sheep, cows, calves, and other large animals that were injured. When winter came, in the icy weather, it had more work than one ambulance could handle. Henry hoped that before many years passed, he could get a second one.

Now when he went about the town, Bergh could see signs of his work's progress.

There were no sick, abandoned animals in the streets. The practice of dumping sheep and calves in carts, helter-skelter, had completely disappeared. The Society had put up drinking fountains so that animals need not suffer from thirst. Some of them were triple fountains—a large trough for horses; beneath that a small basin with fresh, cool water for dogs and cats; and, on the opposite side, a faucet with a cup chained beside it where people could get a drink.

When Henry first started the ASPCA, people thought nothing of driving sick and lame horses or forcing horses with painful harness sores to keep on working. Bergh's vigilance and the many arrests lessened these cases year by year.

Someone asked him once how he could tell a

horse was sick a block away or know a horse had a sore hidden beneath his harness. Henry said, "I don't know how. But I can. I sense it if a horse is miserable."

Now when cattle cars came in from the West, there were fewer animals suffering and dying from

thirst. Henry had fought until he got a law passed forcing the railroads to put watering troughs around the cars and fill them at least three times every twenty-four hours.

People no longer kept cows and horses shut up in barns and sheds without anything to eat or drink. Bergh had battled for a law that made it a misdemeanor to leave animals penned up without food and water.

There were many more laws Henry wanted passed, and many big jobs still to be done. But the progress made by the Society was encouraging.

Then one wintry day, early in 1870, Henry came home with the terrible news that a bill attempting to kill the ASPCA had been presented to the state legislature in Albany.

"But who would introduce such a bill?" Matilda cried. "Remember, the police arrested a man named Mike Burns on a cruelty charge about a year ago? He was found guilty and fined. Mike's been elected to the state legislature since his arrest. This is his revenge."

"But surely if members of the legislature know it's a spite bill they won't dare vote for it," Matilda said.

"One of Mike's more intelligent friends had that same idea, my dear. He has introduced an amendment that does not completely kill our organization, but cripples it so badly, by taking our powers away, that we won't be able to function. Mike's clumsy bill we could beat. But this amendment is much more subtle."

"I suppose you will go to Albany and start fighting?"

"No," Henry said thoughtfully, "I believe I'll ask Elbridge Gerry to go. He's a clever lawyer and a brilliant speaker. I'll take charge of the battle line here."

The plan of campaign was drawn swiftly.

James Gordon Bennett's <u>New York Herald</u> at once came out against Bergh and in favor of the bill. Other papers took it up, and the war was on.

The densely populated lower East Side—still angry at Bergh for stopping the dog fights—demanded that its legislators back the bill. The street railways, always against the ASPCA, were delighted to use all the influence they had to try to force the bill through.

In addition to these, Henry had made many bitter and powerful enemies in the past year fighting the sale of swill milk. The milk came from filthy dairies. The cows were so diseased that many of them had to be supported by slings while being milked. The dairy owners, greedy for profits, fed the animals on poisonous swill left over in beer-making and bought cheaply from the breweries. The milk from these cows was not fit to drink.

Henry's campaign against this practice had brought down on him the wrath of the dairymen who profited by it and the anger of the brewery owners who made a little extra money selling the swill.

These men were determined to get the bill passed and see Bergh defeated, out of their way, once and for all! The tiny ASPCA office was a whirlwind of activity, and the Bergh home was almost never dark. Henry wrote answers to newspaper attacks, prepared articles, sent off letters by the bale, made speeches, and begged for help from everyone he knew.

It was a dark day when Elbridge Gerry sent word from Albany that the bill had passed the lower House.

"If it carries the Senate, that is the end," Henry said to Matilda.

But it did not carry the Senate. Gerry came back to tell them it had failed to pass by only two votes.

This was a slim victory. It showed how uncertain the life of the Society was, how strong its enemies were. Some of those enemies would be even more bitter now because their bill had been defeated.

People made well-meant suggestions to Bergh: "Why don't you quiet down your activities for a while. . . . Stop antagonizing the big interests like the street railways, until this bill is somewhat forgotten."

But Henry said "No!"

He had definite plans for how to handle these "big interests." The fights were sure to come. Delay was useless. He would start with the railways.

EIGHT

ONE MAN TRAFFIC JAM

Late one February afternoon, Henry Bergh left his office and started downtown. He was setting out to create the greatest traffic jam New York City had ever seen.

He was sorry for the working people who would be inconvenienced by it. But in his war with the street railways the time had come for him to strike. Bergh's fight with them had been a losing one so far. First he had gone to the company officials and pleaded for better treatment of the horses.

These men did not deny Bergh's accusations. They knew the conditions he described were true. Scrawny horses were made to pull loads so heavy the animals often could go only a few steps, then stop, trembling, for a moment's rest. Beasts were so dopey with fatigue they were insensible to the driver's voice or his whip, and could be roused after a stop only by the loud jangle of a starting bell. Horses that were sick and lame were driven, driven until they died.

Horses were cheap. Their lives were short at best. What did Bergh want the men to do?

"Put on more cars, more horses," Bergh answered. "Stop this brutal overloading."

"Bah! You can't mix business with sentiment, Bergh. We're running these street railways to make money—and we know how to do it!" They dismissed him.

Next Henry tried to get a law passed limiting the number of passengers allowed on a car and requiring an extra horse at the steepest hills.

But the wealthy railways hired lobbyists—men who went to Albany to threaten, argue, or bribe legislators into voting against the law. The law was not passed.

Henry lamented, "If only horses could lobby, and animals could vote!"

In desperation Bergh began arresting the drivers of overloaded cars, although he knew it was not the fault of these workmen. They were following orders.

This, too, was futile. Many of the judges owned stock in the street railways and dismissed the cases. When a driver was fined, the wealthy company paid the fine as a routine matter. Overloading was so profitable they could well afford to pay an occasional penalty.

Bergh walked on, now, down Broadway toward the Bowery. It was a bad day, with sharp, new snow driven by a north wind. Beneath the heavy cover of old snow lay a glassy sheeting of ice.

Henry noticed, as he walked along, that the street railways, with their usual insolent independence, had cleared the tracks by simply shoveling the snow to the side. It was piled in high drifts, making it impossible for some people to reach their doorways from the street. It left no room, in many streets, for private carriages to stop, and completely covered the hitching posts, spilling over on the sidewalks. But the city officials closed their eyes to this because the street railways were too influential in politics to be antagonized.

At the corner of Bowery and Spring Streets, Henry stopped. It was five o'clock and almost dark. The storm still raged.

A few people were straggling out of shops and offices, starting home early, and the cars were already overloaded. By around six o'clock, thousands of workers would pour out of the large downtown buildings, fill the streets, and clamor for space on the Third Avenue cars. Then the overloading would really be bad.

Henry tried first appealing to the drivers.

"Your load is as heavy now as your horses can pull," he pointed out. "Will you please not permit any more passengers to board this crowded car?"

"Who do you think I am? Vanderbilt? . . . I gotta take my orders from the boss, not you!"

Henry knew, alas, that this was true. He made another request, "Won't you please ask the company to provide an extra team in weather like this to pull through the drifts and up the icy hills?"

"Ask for an extra horse! Gad! Do you want me to lose my job, man?"

Henry had expected answers such as these. It did no good to arrest the drivers or argue with the passengers. He had to give the companies a jolt.

It was just six o'clock when the first heavily overloaded car came toward him. He could hear the tortured breathing of the horses before he saw the car.

People were crushed inside until there was not an inch of space left. They clung to the outside wherever they could catch hold, and they packed onto the steps. A car built to carry twenty-four passengers was loaded with at least a hundred. There would be scores more like this.

Henry watched the poor horses pull a few steps, then halt, strain, and pull a little further.

Calmly he walked out onto the track and stopped the car. Before the driver knew what was happening, he tied the horses to an awning pole.

To the driver he said, "If you make any attempt to move this car until I give you permission, you will be arrested." And then, to the passengers, "If you want to get out and walk, that is your privilege."

A second car had already piled up behind the first one, and another one behind that. Henry knew that as soon as the starters, stationed at City Hall, learned of the traffic snarl, they would reroute their cars by way of Grand Street. So, after warning the driver once more not to start his car, Bergh walked over to Grand.

There he stopped a heavily loaded car and tied the horses to a hitching post. In just a few minutes, traffic began to pile up badly there too. There was no other line now over which the cars could be rerouted.

By the time Henry returned to Spring Street, all of lower New York was becoming one vast traffic jam. Carriages, wagons, and carts were sandwiched in between the stalled cars—the snow piled in the streets made it impossible for them to pass. Teamsters

came, cursing, to see what was wrong. The shouts of the people in the motionless conveyances made a rumbling din.

"What's holding us up? . . . What's the matter?" For blocks back the questions were yelled.

"It's Bergh." The answer was relayed from car to car.

The passengers did not want to get out in the storm and trudge through the ice and snow. Most of them thought that before long Bergh would relent and let the horses go on.

But he stood there, frosted with snow, as stormy as the night, firm and determined.

Gradually, as the hour grew late, however, people began to leave the cold cars to search for some other means of transportation. When enough people got off each car so the horses could pull it without straining, Henry permitted it to go.

But as each started off, Bergh warned the driver that on his return the car must have four horses instead of two to pull it through the icy, snowblocked streets.

"You may tell your superiors, there will be no end to this traffic jam unless they put four horses on every car," he said.

Henry stood there until the cars returned.

He saw them coming, rolling easily, drawn by two teams! Bergh had won a victory over the car companies. Not in court, but on a street corner.

The next day the papers carried big stories on the traffic jam. Some, as always, were against him, and printed such headlines as "Bergh on a Bender" and "Five Thousand People Go without Dinner to Oblige Bergh."

Others approved of his stand against the street railroads, and The Evening Mail went so far as to call him "The Good Genius of the Storm."

He had given the street railways the scare they needed. The tie-up had cost the Third Avenue Line a good many dollars. It had also made a great many customers angry at the railways. People said, "We pay our fares. The lines are making lots of money. Why don't they put on more cars and more horses?"

While the railways didn't care about the horses, the loss of money and business was serious. They realized now they would have to pay some attention to Bergh's demands.

Not long after this victory, New York was given a tragic lesson in the importance of the horse.

An epidemic, called the epizootic, struck the horses of the city. Few of them escaped the illness. Thousands died. Many thousands of others were too ill to work, and the scarcity of the animals proved a great hardship to humans.

Men pulled light cars and wagons. Milk and other liquids were carried in buckets hung on poles. Teams of oxen, brought down from the country, appeared on Broadway. A truckman with a pair of healthy horses could charge fifty dollars a load, and get it. A hansom-cab driver with a horse that had escaped the plague often got ten and fifteen dollars for driving a man a few miles.

The wharves and railroad yards were piled high with goods that could not be moved. Stores ran out of stock. They could not make deliveries. The mail was late. Many people were unable to get to work.

Bergh and his helpers worked night and day caring for the sick horses, putting the hopeless cases out of their misery. The ambulance was busy all the time.

When this sad period was over, Henry found that he and the ASPCA had won hundreds of new friends because of their tireless efforts to help the animals during the epidemic.

The Society was growing steadily now. But one thing it needed desperately was more room. As the Society expanded, the tiny crowded office seemed to shrink.

Henry's dream was for the ASPCA to have a building all its own, but he knew that would cost a great deal of money.

"We'll have it," Matilda encouraged him. "You wait and see. It will come from somewhere."

The society made many friends through helping horses in the epidemic.

NINE

LOUIS BONARD AND HIS WILL

Henry was puzzled by a message delivered to him late one night. It said that a man named Louis Bonard, lying dangerously ill in St. Vincent's Hospital, wanted to see him at once. Bergh had never heard of Louis Bonard.

In spite of the hour, and the fact that it was cold and wintry out, Henry hurried to the hospital.

The man who lay in the narrow white bed was a stranger to him. His face could almost be called ugly. Yet, in it Henry saw something fine and sensitive.

Bonard first spoke quietly and briefly about his life. He told Bergh that he was a Frenchman, from Rouen, who had come to the United States and earned a living trading with the Indians. Later, in New York City, he bought and sold real estate and made a small fortune.

"I have always been interested in your work," he

said, "although I have never done anything to help you. I know I have not long to live, and I have neither family nor friends. I want a will drawn up, leaving my money and property to your ASPCA. I believe it will amount to about $150,000."

During the short while that Bonard lived, Henry frequently visited the lonely man. Several times he went to the modest room Bonard called home to get things the sick man wanted at the hospital. Bergh was, undoubtedly, a great comfort to him during his last days.

When Bonard died, Henry saw that he had a decent burial and made plans for erecting a suitable monument to the man who was the ASPCA's first large benefactor.

As steps were being taken to have Bonard's money transferred to the ASPCA, Henry remarked to Matilda, "This is the first time anything has come easily to the Society. All else we've ever gained, we have had to fight for."

Little did either of them realize what a battle they were to have over the Bonard will!

Shortly after the terms of the bequest became known, an unscrupulous lawyer announced that he had heard from relatives of Bonard's in France who claimed the money was rightfully theirs. He was going to break the will, and see that the nieces and nephews in Rouen got the money.

Henry was quite sure the nieces and nephews lived only in the lawyer's imagination. Bonard had told him he had no family. But the ASPCA could not touch the money until the case was settled.

In the meantime, the French Consul in New York decided that since Bonard was a Frenchman, the money should be claimed for his nation instead of being given to an organization in the United States.

So the court battles began!

Bonard had been a recluse. Nobody knew him. Neighbors seeing him come and go, silent and alone, thought him strange. Now that he was dead, it was easy for greedy lawyers to dig up strange rumors about him and tell them for facts. If they could prove he was crazy when he willed his money to the ASPCA, the will would be just a worthless scrap of paper.

Oh, the stories they told!

"Of course he was crazy," some said, "he was a miser. He lived in a tiny, dirty room, scarcely bigger than a box, behind a tenement, with nothing in it but a broken table and a filthy mattress. A man with all his money wouldn't do that unless he was a lunatic; would he?"

Henry had been to Bonard's room. It was a comfortable room, clean and simply furnished, in a nice brick house. But there were people to swear Bergh lied.

"And why shouldn't Bergh lie? With all that money at stake!" others said. "Besides, I've seen Bonard's room. The door had eight different locks on it, in addition to heavy iron bars. He was a crazy old miser—scared of being robbed."

"Sure he was crazy," the stories grew, "he kept trunks full of gold and silver watches, and boxes of old papers that he guarded in his room."

As further evidence of Bonard's insanity, the lawyers argued that he had a strange kind of religion. "Believed in transmigration of souls," they said.

"Yes. He thought when men died they came back to earth in the form of animals," people who had never heard of Bonard before said knowingly. "That's why he wanted to help the ASPCA. Crazy old fool thought he was coming back as a car horse."

Such ignorant, stupid statements sickened Bergh. He had talked to Bonard about his life, his religion, and his beliefs. He knew that all these people lied.

For nearly two years, the case was battled back and forth in the courts. Sometimes Henry despaired of ever clearing Bonard's name and settling the case as the dead man would have wished it settled.

Finally, on November 8, 1872, the courts decided Bonard had been sane and that the ASPCA should have the money.

During the many months the case had dragged on, the money had dwindled. More than $30,000 was lost in the litigation. Bergh thought it was fair to give $2,500 to St. Vincent's Hospital, where Bonard had been cared for. And the Society had already spent $2,000 for the granite memorial erected in his honor.

However, there was still plenty left for the dreamed-of new building. The building chosen was one of brownstone and brick that stood on the corner of Fourth Avenue and Twenty-second Street. It was a solid, four-story house, and exactly what Henry wanted. It cost $40,000.

A life-size iron horse, painted white, was placed on top of the portico at the entrance as a kind of symbol. In front of the building, the ASPCA erected a drinking fountain so that no animal would ever go by its doors thirsty. It was a gala day when the building was opened. Hundreds of people walked through to admire the spacious, handsome new quarters.

Half the first floor had been remodeled to make room for horse ambulances—there were two of them now. On the first floor, too, was a large room that Henry called "The Chamber of Horrors." Here on display for all to see were bit burrs removed from horses' mouths, clubs taken away from horse-beaters, a stuffed dog rescued too late from a Water Street dog fight, sharp-tipped sticks used by drovers, and many other proofs of cruelty.

The rest of the building was divided into offices, meeting rooms, and much-needed storage space.

At the end of that first day, after all the visitors had gone, Henry and Matilda stood in his new office, looking out the window. From the window they could see up and down busy Fourth Avenue, across the side street to Broadway.

"With all the space here, Henry, so much more can be done . . . ."

But Henry whirled suddenly from the window, snatched his hat and cane, and was off in a flash.

Matilda noticed then, coming down the Avenue, a cab drawn by a horse that limped badly.

She smiled to see Henry dash for the cab, the cab stop, the driver climb down. She heard the shouts of the irate passenger, the driver's explanations.

"Yes," said Matilda as she watched, "he will enjoy his new office very much. It has a lovely view."

TEN

BERGH AND BARNUM

Henry walked between the rows of caged animals and spoke angrily to the fat man beside him. "I warn you, Barnum, you're going to have another disastrous fire here. This wooden building is flimsy as a packing-box—and animals in heavy cages on all three floors!"

"The way I keep the animals in this Museum is my business," Barnum shouted above the noise of the crowd of spectators visiting the museum. "Look at the straw on the floors here—a flick of cigar ash could ignite it. And those partitions trimmed with paper streamers," Henry raised his cane and pointed to the thin wooden walls. "The least you could do is put your cages on wheels so some of the animals might be rescued."

"I know how to run a menagerie, Bergh. You're a snooping old fool."

"And you're a fraud, Barnum, who will do

anything for money."

From the earliest days of the ASPCA, Henry had trouble with P. T. Barnum and his Museum.

Now as he was about to leave the building, Bergh noticed a large crowd pushing around the cage that housed the anaconda. It seemed a lot of attention for one snake to get, and Henry went over to investigate.

When he was able to get to the cage, he saw the large snake lying quietly in one corner. But running frantically around on the floor was a small, frightened rabbit, and a pair of doves beat against the sides of the cage, trying desperately to escape.

The people waited, breathlessly excited, for the snake to pounce on the terrified creatures.

Henry knew it might be weeks before the snake would make any move toward the rabbit or birds. The anaconda eats only when it is hungry, and often a month or more goes by between meals.

In the meantime, however, Barnum was profiting by the terror of the doves and the rabbit. People were paying admission, flocking to the cage, expecting any moment to see the anaconda strike.

Bergh could not compel Barnum to abandon his firetrap building. He could not prevent him from hoodwinking the public. But he could force him, under the anti-cruelty law, to release the frightened creatures that were being kept needlessly in the cage and made to suffer for Barnum's gain.

Barnum roared, "You don't know anything about snakes! Anacondas will eat only live food they catch themselves. You want me to let my snake starve to death?"

"That anaconda isn't even hungry," Bergh answered. "You are cruelly keeping the rabbit and birds in there just to draw a crowd, to make money. If they aren't taken out at once, I'll have you arrested." The next day the snake was alone in the cage. As the weeks and months went by, Henry and others too wondered where and how the anaconda was being fed.

One day a newspaper reporter came into Bergh's office.

"Barnum's snake," he said, "is now boarding at the Taylor Hotel, across the river in Jersey City. I thought you might be interested."

"The Taylor Hotel?" Henry waited for the newspaperman to explain.

The reporter told how he had gone over to the hotel the night before with one of Barnum's men. They had taken the snake, locked in a large suitcase, with them.

At the hotel they went to a room, closed the doors and windows and drew the shades. In the meantime, a number of small animals had been released in the room.

The attendant and the reporter wrapped themselves from head to foot in blankets and climbed up onto a bed to watch. The lock of the suitcase was released by means of a string attachment, and a moment later the anaconda glided out.

"It was a beautiful creature," the reporter described it, "shimmering and graceful, silvery against the flowered Brussels carpet. And believe me, Mr. Bergh, I am sure the little animals felt no pain. They showed no fright, and the feast was over so quickly, I don't think they ever knew what struck them."

After the meal, the snake was sluggish and harmless. The attendant stuffed it into the suitcase and carried it back to its cage in New York.

Henry realized it was true that some snakes—including anacondas and boa constrictors—would eat only live food they had caught themselves, and without it, of course, they would starve to death. But he had objected to Barnum's commercializing this fact.

Now he and Barnum compromised. Bergh

agreed to allow him to feed the snake if it was done at night, privately, after the Museum had closed.

This compromise, however, did not make friends of Bergh and Barnum. Henry kept strict vigilance over the Museum. He found animals locked in cages so small they could not stand up. With the threat of arrest, he forced Barnum to move the beasts out of these cramped cages into roomier quarters. He checked on attendants who mistreated animals and investigated to make sure there was sufficient water, food, and ventilation.

One night as Henry was leaving the Museum, he saw a poster advertising a coming attraction. In lurid colors the poster pictured a horse called Salamander, the Fire Horse, stepping through a flaming hoop.

Henry said, "If it **is** fire, the horse will be burned, and that's cruelty. This must be investigated."

Bergh let it be known publicly that on a certain night Salamander's act was to be investigated by the ASPCA. If the horse was burned, the exhibition would be stopped, and Barnum would be arrested. The audience watched tensely as Salamander walked through the circles of fire. When the act was over, Barnum himself hurried out to make a curtain speech.

He said, "Friends, I have been catering to public

amusement for forty-eight years, yet I am here today expecting arrest and imprisonment." His voice was that of a martyr. His face with its bulbous nose and broad round chin was grieved. "Either Mr. Bergh or I must run this show and for the present I intend to. . . ."

Then to prove that Salamander could not be harmed by the act, Mr. Barnum himself walked through the flaming hoops, and came out unscorched.

"Oh, it isn't fire at all," people in the audience whispered in disgust. "We've been fooled . . . it's all a fake . . . it's another Barnum humbug. . . ."

Henry chuckled, "It's a humbug all right! Barnum proved he was innocent of any cruelty charge, but he has made a lot of people angry."

During all this time, Henry continued to warn Barnum of the fire hazards at his Museum, and Barnum stubbornly refused to listen. On a zero night in early March, Bergh's prophecy of disaster came true.

It was shortly after midnight when Henry was wakened by the sound of running footsteps and heard someone shout, "Barnum's Museum's on fire!" He dressed quickly and hurried out. He could see a red glow starting to stain the sky, and he knew the fire was rapidly getting out of control.

Henry reached the Museum in time to hear the first terrible cries of trapped animals. The flames had enveloped the first two floors, and firemen were pouring great streams of water onto the building in a desperate attempt to keep the blaze from spreading to the third.

The ever-moving crowds gathered on Broadway to watch. The people were nervous and panicky lest some wild animals escape. Confusion increased as they rushed down the side streets each time an especially sharp cry was heard.

When the fat lady and the giantess, in scanty attire, came screaming out of the stage entrance, firemen and police dived into the open door and dragged out a zebra, two camels, a giraffe, and some cages of small birds. They smashed in the front door and led out a kangaroo, two pelicans, a frightened silver pheasant. These were huddled in their cages on the sidewalk, a sad and pitifully small collection. In the broiling flames no other rescues were possible.

The animal noises were quieting when suddenly a high flame leapt up, throwing light and heat into the top floor where lions, tigers, and bears were caged. Henry heard their great roars and the sounds of them beating against their cages.

One beautiful Bengal tiger did escape. But while

the crowds fled in terror, firemen held her at bay with a hose, and a policeman shot her.

Henry stayed—hoping he might be able to help—until the last flame was gone and the smoke a mere smudge in the sky. It was almost daylight. The building was a black shell, and in the bitter cold the water from the fire hoses had frozen against it in glittering, silver cascades.

Bergh turned toward home. His heart was filled with pity for the poor animals and a deep anger at Barnum.

"I suppose he's learned his lesson, Matilda," Henry said as he told her of the fire. "At the expense of helpless caged creatures. What a price!"

As a matter of fact, Barnum had not learned his lesson. He gathered a new collection of animals and put them in another flimsy building. On a Christmas Eve, less than four years later, the Museum burned again.

After that fire, Barnum realized that Bergh's pleas for fire prevention must be heeded. He had a new building erected, as fireproof as possible, equipped with movable cages, and invited Henry to come and inspect it.

Bergh approved of the building. But as he walked around with Barnum he stopped once to

scold a bareback rider for lashing a horse with the butt of a whip. He called Barnum's attention threateningly to the burns on an elephant's hide. He demanded that a hyena be tied with a longer tether.

When he left he smiled and said, "Your new building is all right, Barnum. But remember, you are dependent on these dumb beasts for your livelihood. You should be grateful enough to them to see they are treated well. I'll be back."

Barnum scowled as he watched the tall, well-dressed man walk briskly away. Yes, he would be back. Barnum knew that. Resigned, he went to obey Bergh's order, to lengthen the hyena's tether.

ELEVEN

THOUSANDS OF DOGS

"Can you help us, please, Mr. Bergh?" A little girl came into Henry's office one hot July day. "Our puppy is gone and we're afraid some boys have stolen him to sell to the Pound."

With the child was her younger brother, his eyes swollen from crying, his face stained with tears. At her mention of the Pound, the boy began to cry again.

Henry said comfortingly, "Dry your eyes now. You sit here for a few minutes and as soon as I get these papers finished I will help you find your dog."

Theirs was an old story to Henry, and a sad one. The Dog Pound was one of the shames of the city. Because of a mistaken but popular belief that hot weather caused dogs to go mad, the City offered, during the summer, fifty cents apiece for any stray dog taken to the Pound.

No dog in New York was safe. Boys snatched them off the streets and out of yards. They stole them from porches and doorways. At the Pound, dogs were held until late afternoon. Then those that were not claimed by their owners were drowned. Often owners did not miss their pets until it was too late. Furthermore, it cost two dollars to have a dog released, and sometimes even though their pets were found at the Pound, the owners did not have the money to get them.

The Pound keeper was usually a hard, brutal man, and a petty racketeer. When a particularly fine, pedigreed dog was brought in, he would hold it aside and demand a reward from the owner who came to claim the animal.

One gentleman reported to Bergh that his valuable Newfoundland puppy had been stolen eleven times in five weeks—and retrieved each time at the Pound only after he had paid the keeper money.

Bergh finished his work quickly, put the two children in a carriage, and drove to the Pound.

The Pound was an old shed over by the East River. It could hardly be called a building, for there was no roof over part of it and no floor but the earth. The dogs were tied by short ropes to low railings, so close together that they fought constantly.

As soon as Henry and the children came in, all the dogs leapt up as far as their short tethers would allow, jumping and barking and straining. Each, in his great excitement and eagerness, seemed to hope someone had come to rescue him and take him home.

In this bedlam, the children and Bergh walked up and down the rows. While they were searching, Henry noticed three ragged urchins run into the Pound, each dragging two dogs. The Pound keeper gave them a dollar apiece in exchange for the dogs, and the boys ran off, probably to catch more animals. As always, this sight saddened Henry. Not only did he feel sorry for the unfortunate dogs, but, worse than that, he knew this practice was making thieves of many children.

Suddenly the little girl and her brother gave a shout of joy. Henry saw them reach for a little fluffy white dog that jumped frantically to get loose. They had found their puppy.

Henry knew the children had no money. He took two dollars from his pocket and paid the keeper.

The keeper gave Henry a sneering grin. "Don'tcha get tired of payin' for other people's mutts?" He thought Henry was crazy, buying back dogs for people who couldn't afford to redeem them.

He thought Henry was crazy, too, because he was always trying to get the keeper to provide pans of cool water for the thirsty animals.

"They'll get plenty of water tonight, mister," he would laugh at Henry.

That day Bergh left determined to do something at once about the city Dog Pound.

First he went to the Mayor. He asked the Mayor to help him get an ordinance passed which would discourage children from stealing dogs and selling them to the Pound.

When the law was passed, it prohibited anyone under eighteen years old from bringing in a dog. It also reduced the price paid from fifty to twenty-five cents, thus making the practice much less profitable.

There are always a few people who try to beat the law. Henry was disgusted, now, to see dishonest men, small-time racketeers, become "dog brokers." They had children get the dogs and turn the animals over to them. The men then took the dogs to the Pound, collected their twenty-five cents bounty on each and gave the children part of the money. It was not uncommon for a "dog broker" to take in twenty or thirty animals at a time day after day.

This crooked game did not last long, however. Boys were not willing to risk stealing an animal for a paltry ten or fifteen cents. The "brokers," too, were easily caught.

There was a sharp drop in the number of dogs taken to the Pound after this. Before the law was in effect, around six thousand dogs were handled there each summer. Under the new law, the number dwindled to less than a thousand.

With this accomplished, Henry began a campaign to get better quarters and kinder treatment for the animals at the Pound.

He realized that most people never saw the Pound and did not know how bad the conditions were. Henry asked newspapermen to visit it and write about it for their papers. Many of them did. Some of the stories were illustrated with drawings that pictured the abuses of the Pound.

These roused a few people to join Bergh in his campaign for a new Dog Pound, and gradually the movement gathered weight. There were always some

who opposed anything he did. One paper printed a cartoon of Henry weeping, following a wagonload of dogs headed for the Pound. It was labeled, "The Only Mourner."

Although Bergh was able to better conditions at the Pound a little each summer, it took him eight years of fighting to get the kind of Dog Pound he wanted. It was a clean, well-ventilated building with rows of stalls. Each dog had a stall to himself, with enough room for comfort, straw to lie on, and a pan of fresh water. Money was appropriated for feeding the animals, and care was taken to employ kind and responsible keepers. Eventually the city hired dogcatchers instead of paying people for bringing in the animals.

When the new Dog Pound was opened, the public was very proud of it, and the city boasted that nowhere in America was there a finer one. Few people, however, gave any thought to the long battle Bergh had waged to get it built.

During the time Henry had worked for reforms at the Pound he had, of course, been busy with many other things.

Every year his fight with the railroads and shipping companies over the transportation of cattle intensified. The water-troughs that had been made compulsory in cattle cars saved beasts from dying of thirst. But that reform was not enough. Henry saw the unventilated cars come in with as many as twenty animals dead of suffocation. Packed in for days without food, they trampled one another, kicked and butted, so that those which did not die were painfully injured. Everywhere—off the cars, down the yards, onto ships—men prodded and gouged them with sticks tipped with pointed metal blades. These abuses Henry fought to stop.

More than once in cold weather Bergh had held up the sailing of a ship because cattle were crowded on open decks for the long, rough journey across the North Atlantic.

Henry was appalled by the very waste of it, as well as the cruelty.

But the shippers' attitude was to let them freeze to death, or crush each other in the storms. Out West, the bright, new, fertile West, there were plenty more to replace them.

Henry was still battling the street railways, too. There was, for example, the matter of their salting the streets in the winter in order to melt the ice and snow. Because salt lowers the freezing temperature of water, the horses that had to walk and stand in the salty slush often had their feet frozen. Hundreds died every winter from this exposure.

Even worse, Henry learned, children who crossed these streets on their way to school suffered chills from the extremely cold salted water. But the street railways found this the cheapest way of clearing their tracks.

Each winter, regularly as clockwork, Henry proposed another bill outlawing the street saltings. Year after year he was defeated. Not until 1878—when the Society was twelve years old—did he finally get it passed.

There was the matter, too, of stable fires. Hundreds of horses were stabled on the second and third floors of wooden buildings, tied to their stalls so there was no possible escape. Three hundred perished in one night's blaze.

Henry tried to get the companies to stable their horses on the ground floors of buildings. But it was more convenient to leave the cars and wagons there, and drive the horses up a ramp to the floors above.

He suggested the use of a device which made it possible, by pulling a central lever, to release the halters in each stall at the same time, thus giving the horses at least a chance to escape. He invented "blinds" which stable hands could fit over horses' eyes at the first sign of fire so that the animals could be led to safety instead of becoming panicked. But these devices cost money. Horses were cheap.

Human life, too, was considered cheap. Henry had a great struggle trying to get fire laws passed. He had, himself, been through a tragic fire, when the steamer <u>Henry Clay</u> burned with eighty lives lost. He knew what horrible things fires were and how easily many of them could be prevented.

He wanted theater owners prohibited from blocking the aisles with chairs. He wanted exits marked so theaters could be emptied more efficiently in case of fire. He wanted tenements to be equipped with fire escapes. For a long time when he spoke of these things, people said, "Oh, Bergh is sounding off again! He's cracked!" Bergh owned a tenement building in New York. It boasted the first fire escape in New York City. People walked blocks to look at it—and to laugh.

Henry was still fighting the pigeon shoots, the swill milk racket, the unsanitary conditions in slaughterhouses. He was inventing a sling-and-derrick contraption that would make it possible to rescue horses that fell in excavations and gullies. Oh, he was very busy.

Many times when Matilda reviewed all the burdens Henry was shouldering she would say, "I pray and hope he discovers nothing else that needs his attention. He scarcely finds time to sleep as it is."

But one evening Henry came home and said to his wife, "Matilda, do you think a child could, justifiably, be considered a little animal?"

"Why, I don't know, Henry. That's an odd question."

"A woman came to me today to ask for help," Henry said. "I want to tell you what she told me. . . ."

Henry began, then, to tell Matilda a story, the story of a child.

Now healthy animals are kept at the Pound and new owners found for them.

TWELVE

THE CHILD NAMED MARY ELLEN

The woman who came in to tell Henry Bergh about the child introduced herself as Mrs. Wheeler. Henry saw at once that she was greatly troubled.

"You are my last resort for help, Mr. Bergh," she said. "If you can't help me, I'm sure I don't know who will."

Then she told Henry this story:

While visiting in a poor section of the city, about three months earlier, Mrs. Wheeler had heard rumors that a child was being kept imprisoned in a tenement flat. Neighbors said that in two years they had seen the little girl only once, and then just for a moment when the door was left ajar. They knew she was there, however, for they heard her crying and the loud scolding of the woman who was apparently her guardian. The woman was cross and unfriendly to all who came to her door and allowed no one to enter the flat.

Mrs. Wheeler decided to do some detective work.

First she went to see the people who lived upstairs in the same tenement—a young man and his invalid wife. They welcomed Mrs. Wheeler when they found she wanted to help the child, for her cries and the knowledge that she was being treated cruelly distressed them greatly. They had never seen the child, but they knew from hearing the woman shout at her that her name was Mary Ellen. They told Mrs. Wheeler they would gladly help in any way they could.

Mrs. Wheeler then tried to gain admission to the flat by knocking on the door and asking the woman if she would help her sick neighbor. The first few times the door was closed in her face. But at last, one stormy winter day, she was allowed to step inside for a few seconds.

Through an open doorway she saw the child, standing on a box at the kitchen sink, washing dishes. She was thin and small, about the size of a five-year old, and white as wax. Though the day was bitter cold, she was barefoot and scantily dressed. There were marks on her arms and legs, and Mrs. Wheeler knew the neighbors' stories of her cruel treatment were only too true. On the table was a heavy whip.

Mrs. Wheeler outwardly showed no interest in the child, and she was pleasant to the woman when told to leave. She did not want to arouse any suspicions while Mary Ellen was still there. If alarmed, the woman might hide the child or move.

She went, at once, to the police with her story. To her dismay she found they could not help her. The child was owned by her guardian, she was told. The city had no right to interfere.

Next she went to the Children's Aid Society. But it, too, had no legal means of helping the child. On request, it could feed a hungry child or give clothes to the poor, but it could do nothing for a child who was being mistreated.

Mrs. Wheeler then went to the heads of orphanages to see if they could take the child. They were powerless in such a case. They could claim children that had been abandoned or orphaned, but Mary Ellen had a guardian.

For three months Mrs. Wheeler tried to find somebody with authority to rescue the child, but without success.

"Now, in desperation, I have come to you," she said to Henry when she finished her story. "The law prohibits cruelty to any animal. Your Society fights to see that this law is enforced. This child **is** a little animal. Can't your Society protect her?"

Henry was silent in thought for several minutes. When he spoke he said, "I would like to help in this case. But, you know, definite testimony is necessary before one dares interfere between a child and a person claiming guardianship. Will you send me a written statement? And allow me a little time to consider whether or not the ASPCA has the legal right to help this child?"

That night, as Henry told Mary Ellen's story to Matilda, they thought of the many times Bergh had been criticized for working in behalf of animals instead of humans.

Over and over he had heard, "If you'd put your time and energy into trying to help **people** instead of dumb animals, you'd be accomplishing something. You rescue dogs and horses while children starve."

It was difficult for Bergh to make these critics understand that while he realized something should be done to help children, **he** had set out to do another job. And that job was consuming all of his time and energy and much of his money.

Once—three years before he first heard of Mary Ellen—Bergh did intercede in the case of a child who was being mistreated as a household drudge. He pleaded her cause in court, and succeeded in having her taken away from her cruel guardian and sent to her grandmother.

At that time he was tempted to go on with the work of helping children. But he was busy with so many responsibilities, he felt he could not do justice to this new large task.

He hoped that some other man or woman, or perhaps a children's welfare society, might become interested in fighting for the legal rights for children that he had secured for animals. But no one did.

Henry knew now there was no use wishing or waiting for someone else to come to Mary Ellen's rescue. He decided, after talking it over with Matilda, to take action at once.

But first of all, before the case could be taken to court, he must have more evidence that the child was actually mistreated. He needed additional testimony.

The next morning he called in an ASPCA agent and handed the man a slip of paper and a thick record book.

"Go to this address," Henry directed him, "and tell the woman who answers the door that you are a census taker. Insist that she let you in while you ask a few questions."

Henry then rapidly outlined the purpose of this ruse, and sent the "census taker" on his way. When the man returned he reported to Henry that he too had seen the child. She was a pitiful sight. Everything Mrs. Wheeler had said was true.

With this evidence, Bergh told the story of Mary Ellen to a Supreme Court judge, and got a writ of *habeas corpus* which allowed him to take the little girl from her guardian and bring her into court.

Since the child wore no clothes but a tattered summer dress, and the day in late March was chilly, she was brought into court wrapped in a horse blanket.

They carried her in, screaming and shrieking with fright, for no one had ever been kind to her before, and she could not understand that these people offered help. When a policeman gave her a stick of peppermint, hoping to quiet her, she thought it was something to hit her with and struck him. She had never seen candy.

As they set her down before the bench, the child crawled deep into the blanket as if to hide. She hushed now and waited, trembling.

Henry spoke: "Your Honor, I represent the American Society for the Prevention of Cruelty to Animals. This child is an animal . . . a human animal. If there is no justice for her as a child, then let us at least give her the rights we would give a dog in the street. . . ."

When Bergh finished speaking, and the testimony had been given, the judge said, "Unwrap the child, so that the court may see her condition."

Gently, Bergh unwrapped the frightened child. The judge took one look at the poor, mistreated little body and turned away. "That is evidence enough," he said.

He then sentenced her guardian to prison for one year and directed that Mary Ellen be turned over to "The Sheltering Arms," a children's home.

Henry took twenty-five dollars from his pocket and gave it to Mrs. Wheeler so she could buy the child some clothes.

Mary Ellen had many things to learn, and the judge wisely thought she would learn them more easily in a home with other children. She had never talked to another child. She had never seen a toy. She had to learn to walk on the ground, because, having walked only on floors, she could not understand uneven surfaces. Though she looked five and was actually nine, she knew less than many three year-olds.

Mary Ellen learned fast, however, in her new,

healthful surroundings, and after a short while the judge allowed Mrs. Wheeler's sister to adopt her. She grew up to be a happy and attractive woman.

Henry knew, the morning Mary Ellen was carried into court, that the case would cause fresh troubles and more work for him.

At once people flocked to him with stories of other mistreated children—youngsters who were being starved and beaten; boys forced to do men's work for which they were never paid; children who were drugged and made to look deformed by beggars in order to excite the pity of passersby; waifs who had run away from mean guardians and had been living like little animals in hiding along the waterfront. Each day the number of cases reported increased.

Bergh realized that, in order to handle them properly, a separate organization would have to be formed. He and the ASPCA's lawyer, Elbridge Gerry, decided then to found the Society for the Prevention of Cruelty to Children.

It was started in much the same way as the ASPCA. First a Declaration was drawn up and prominent people were asked to sign it. Meetings were held. A charter and laws were prepared. And the next step was to take them to Albany and get the legislature to pass them.

But now, even in work as noble as this, Bergh's enemies began to strike.

They cried, "Bergh's not satisfied with telling us how to treat our animals. Now he wants to tell us how to bring up our children!"

The newspapers jumped into the fight. The New York Sun ran a story violently opposing Bergh's plan for the new Society and called Henry "a man who cannot be happy unless he is either prying into other people's affairs or regulating other people's conduct."

A religious journal published an article headed "Leave Our Children Alone!" and said Bergh's scheme was just a desire to force his own way of life on little children.

To poor Bergh, who had heard so often the jibe, "Instead of bothering with dumb animals, why don't you help children?" this storm of opposition was ironic indeed.

Fortunately a new friend had come to assist Henry and Gerry. His name was John D. Wright. He was a Quaker, a fine gentleman and a fearless fighter. He offered to take the bill and the charter to Albany and get them through the legislature.

It took Wright ten weeks of hard work in Albany to get the charter and new law through. They were passed on April 27, 1875, more than a year after Mary Ellen's case had been taken before the judge.

During that year of fighting to found the Society for the Prevention of Cruelty to Children, Henry had worked hard. He had shouldered the burden of the ASPCA and the children's cases too.

Now that the struggle was over, he placed the new Society in the capable hands of John Wright and Elbridge Gerry.

Bergh was again free to give all his time and effort to his greatest interest—the ASPCA.

Now horses are taken care of in hot weather.

THIRTEEN

THE TWENTIETH ANNIVERSARY

It was a soft April evening in 1886 and the twentieth birthday of Henry Bergh's ASPCA.

Through the spring twilight, Henry and Matilda rode down Fifth Avenue on their way to the annual meeting of the Society.

Matilda said, with a small scold in her voice, "You must have been up **very** early this morning. You were gone when I wakened at five. Are you tired?"

"No," Henry answered, "I'm not tired." He smiled at her. "By five o'clock I was on board a cattle ship, measuring the sizes of stalls, testing the food and water and checking on ventilation. The shippers are being pretty careful nowadays to obey the laws regarding the transportation of livestock. However, if we relaxed our watchfulness, I don't know——"

Even though this day was, to him, an important anniversary, he had spent it much as any other day.

It was still early morning when he left the cattle ship and walked down to the waterfront markets to check the peddlers' horses. The rascals had a trick of starting a lame horse out in the morning and, if caught later in the day, swearing the animal was all right when it left the stable. Henry had to catch them early.

From there he had started walking toward his office. On his way he stopped by a saloon where someone had told him a dog was being used on a treadmill to run a cider press. The poor animal was in the window, the better to attract a crowd. It was thin and worn, and exhausted even at that hour, for it was tied so that if it stopped treading it choked. Henry released the dog and arrested the owner.

He was at his office by ten.

Waiting for him was a frightened boy with a struggling puppy in his arms. The pup, scarcely able to breathe, had a fishbone in its throat. Bergh was practiced at cases like this. Carefully he pulled out the bone, and took time to explain to the young master that he must never feed his dog bony fish or chicken bones.

As the child was leaving, two of the Society's agents came in. Could Mr. Bergh go with them out to Long Island late the following night? After a good deal of detective work they had found that cock fights were being held secretly in a deep woods on the Island. They wanted Henry to help them arrest the scamps. Henry said he would gladly go.

Before the morning was over, Henry had letters to write, visitors to see, finishing touches to make on his speech. He would be expected to give an appropriate talk that night at the annual meeting.

By early afternoon, however, he was miles up-town, at the horse market, investigating conditions there. They were bad, too! And it would take a lot of hard work to better them. The market was crowded with horse traders, peddlers and teamsters, buying and selling beasts for two dollars and up. Old horses, lame horses, sick horses, scarcely any of them fit for work. But traders knew all kinds of tricks! Arsenic, for example, made the horses look temporarily high-spirited and their coats shine brighter. Besides, almost any horse could be made to work for a few weeks, and the sum paid was small.

As Henry recalled the horse market, he wondered if he should tell Matilda, now that he had bought three broken-down old horses himself. Teamsters were bidding for them. He knew that unless he rescued them, they would be auctioned off to someone who would require them to do work they could not stand.

After the horse market, he had stopped in at the East River stock yards, then crossed town to inspect a dairy on the West Side.

So his day had gone! Sometimes he thought the older the Society grew, the more work they found that needed doing.

At the meeting Henry made his speech of welcome. It was brief but eloquent, and Matilda was very proud of him.

The Secretary then rose to give his report. It was deeply gratifying to Bergh that the Society's secretary was his own nephew and namesake.

Together Matilda and Henry sat and listened to the younger man's voice: "More than three-fourths of our nation's states and territories now have anti-cruelty laws. . . . South American countries are forming societies patterned after our own . . . our roll of members at present contains five hundred and fourteen names. . . ."

Yes, it had grown. Henry thought of the first meeting, held on that stormy night with only a handful of men present and violent antagonism to be fought on all sides. Gradually much of that antagonism had been broken down. He smiled now to think of how some of his bitterest enemies had been won over. During the past year, old

P. T. Barnum had actually joined the ASPCA! He had even invited Henry to come up to Bridgeport and visit him. Henry intended to go, too.

The Secretary spoke on, recounting the Society's successes, listing the tasks that still needed to be done. Henry scowled at the mention of pigeon shoots. He'd get that law passed yet! Let the sportsmen laugh at his idea of their using clay pigeons instead of live birds—they'd come to it! People had laughed at many of Bergh's ideas, and lived to accept them.

Pails of water are used to cool horses, and blankets to keep them warm.

When the meeting was over, and Henry and Matilda were home again, she said, "Let's look at the diamond medal!"

It was appropriate on this twentieth anniversary.

Henry was very proud of the medal. The ASPCA had given it to him six years previous as a token of the Society's appreciation.

Unlocking a small wall safe, he lifted out the velvet box and handed it to Matilda. She placed it on the table where the gaslight fell and opened it.

The diamonds in the golden oval sparkled with bursts of color and brilliance. Silently Henry and Matilda read, for the hundredth time or more, the inscription on the medal: "Presented to Henry Bergh by the Executive Committee as a mark of their personal esteem and friendship."

"Twenty years is a large part of your life to give, Henry. Have you ever been sorry?" Matilda asked.

She was thinking of the winter nights he had risen in a blizzard to go out on rescue work. Of the times he had steeled himself to ask people for money when the Society was in need. Of the friends he had lost because of his loyalty to the work and the enemies he had fought. Of the harsh ridicule and misunderstanding. She was thinking, too, that he, a gentle, peace-loving person, had been constantly in the midst of street quarrels, arguments, court battles, fights with law breakers. For twenty years.

"No," Henry answered her question, "I have never been sorry; have you?"

He was thinking of the brilliant social life she had been forced to give up—Matilda, who was beautiful and loved parties and people and pretty clothes. He was remembering the countless nights he had left her alone, when he was out on the Society's work, and how through all those years she had never complained of her loneliness.

"No," Matilda said. "These have been the good years. I have never been sorry."

She smiled up at him, and her white hands reached for the velvet box. She closed it gently and handed it to Henry. Together they walked back to the safe and locked it carefully away.

GLOSSARY

amphibious able to live on land or in the water

anaconda a large snake native to South America

arsenic a type of poison

John Jacob Astor - one of America's wealthiest men in the 18th and 19th centuries

barque this word is also spelled <u>bark</u>; a type of sailing ship with three to five masts; related to the Egyptian word <u>barge</u>

bedlam noisy uproar and confusion

bequest a gift to someone in a person's last will and testament

Edwin Booth - an American actor (1833-1893), brother of John Wilkes Booth who assassinated Abraham Lincoln

brig a type of sailing ship with two masts; this word is short for <u>brigantine</u> which comes from the Italian for "pirate ship"

brocade a richly-designed heavy fabric

"by Jove" a mild oath

caulkers a person whose job is to make something (usually a boat) watertight

confiscated taken away by legal means, usually by the government as a means of punishment

conveyance a vehicle, such as a car or bus

Czar and Czarina - titles for king and queen of Russia

din   a loud noise of many different sounds

dive   a slang word for a run-down bar or club

"douse de glim" - a slang expression meaning "put out the lights"

dray   a low heavy cart without sides used to haul things

drovers   people who drive cattle or sheep

epizootic   an epizootic is when a disease attacks a large numberof animals at once

ferret   to search out or seek

frock coat   a man's dress overcoat with knee-length skirts, worn mainly in the 19th century

Galapagos Tortoise - a type of land-dwelling turtle native to the Galapagos Islands

genial   friendly and pleasant

girder   a horizontal beam supporting a vertical load

goad   to prod someone to do something, sometimes by using a stick

Horace Greeley - an American journalist and political leader (1811-1872)

habeas corpus - a legal term which means to release from unlawful restraint

hansom-cab a two-wheeled covered carriage with the driver above and behind the passengers

hoodwinking - to fool or put something over on someone

infamous   well-known for having done something bad

joiners   carpenters

lavish   extravagant

litigation   legal action or process

lobbyist   a person employed by a certain group to influence legislators to vote for measures favorable to the interest he represents

martyr   one who sacrifices something very important in order to further a belief or cause

menagerie   a group of wild animals on exhibition

misdemeanor - an offense less serious than offenses called felonies. The punishment for misdemeanors is less serious than for felonies.

miser   a very stingy person or someone who hoards his money

monsieur   the French word for "Mister"

naturalist   a person who has a good deal of knowledge about the natural world, plants and animals

packet boat   a type of boat, usually a coastal or river steamer, that has a regular route and carries passengers

racketeer   a person engaged in an illegal business

recluse   a hermit or a person who wants to be by himself all the time

regime   a system of government

scamp   a rascal

schooner   a type of ship with two or more masts

scoundrel   a villainous person, one who isn't very nice

sentimental   excessive emotionalism

sprigged muslin - a type of plain-weave cotton cloth decorated with designs of buds and twigs

swill	a mixture of liquid and solid food or a deep draft of liquor
tantalizing	something a person really wants but cannot have because it is always just out of reach
teamsters	a person who drives a team of horses, or a truck driver
tenement	an apartment building, often run-down
terrapin	a type of aquatic North American turtle
transmigration of souls	- the belief that the soul passes into another body after death
unscrupulous	- under-handed, not caring about what is right or ethical
urchin	a small mischievous boy
Vanderbilt	a wealthy American family founded by Cornelius Vanderbilt (1794-1877)
veranda	a porch or balcony, sometimes having a roof and sometimes partly enclosed
vigilance	watchfulness
waif	a forsaken or orphaned child, or a homeless person
way	one meaning of this word has to do with machinery and refers to a strip of a surface that guides a moving part; in this case, the strips guide the ship into the water
windlass	a type of machine for hauling or lifting, usually made by a rope wound around a drum and turned by a crank